Spirit Freedom

A GUIDE TO SPIRITUALLY PREPARE
THE NEXT GENERATION FOR THE FUTURE

Taloa Walters

First published by Ultimate World Publishing 2020
Copyright © 2020 Taloa Walters

ISBN

Paperback: 978-1-922372-94-9
Ebook: 978-1-922372-95-6

Taloa Walters has asserted her rights under the Copyright, Designs and Patents Act 1988 to be identified as the author of this work. The information in this book is based on the author's experiences and opinions. The publisher specifically disclaims responsibility for any adverse consequences which may result from use of the information contained herein. Permission to use information has been sought by the author. Any breaches will be rectified in further editions of the book.

All rights reserved. No part of this publication may be reproduced, stored in or introduced into a retrieval system, or transmitted in any form, or by any means (electronic, mechanical, photocopying, recording or otherwise) without the prior written permission of the author. Any person who does any unauthorised act in relation to this publication may be liable to criminal prosecution and civil claims for damages. Enquiries should be made through the publisher.

Cover design: Ultimate World Publishing
Layout and typesetting: Ultimate World Publishing
Editor: Hayley Ward
Cover image: PopTika-Shutterstock.com

Ultimate World Publishing
Diamond Creek,
Victoria Australia 3089
www.writeabook.com.au

Dedication

This book is dedicated to our Heavenly Father, our saviour and older brother, Jesus Christ, the Holy Ghost, my daughters, my family and all my friends that I have connected with throughout my life for their unconditional love, kindness, patience and endless support.

Testimonials

Taloa Walters' insightful wisdom sheds hope and light that all things are possible through the strength of the spirit. Her energy, knowledge and enthusiasm provide a hopeful guide that, no matter what challenges or circumstances one faces, there is power in their soul to choose spiritual freedom. A fantastic book that will enlighten the reader to feel the love and guidance of their Creator and stir up passion to live their fullest life possible.

Nikki Langman

Rarely; certainly not often, are we blessed to cross paths with an individual who is truly extraordinary, unique, and even peculiar. These special people make us stop, pay attention, self-reflect; they make us want to be a better us.

One such privilege of mine was on November 5, 1992, with the arrival of Taloa Solitua in Adelaide, Australia to serve her faith at great personal effort, and sacrifice. To begin her mission, I knelt with her as she offered a prayer. The power and sincerity of her words pierced my heart, certifying to me that clearly, this was no ordinary woman. This was a woman of pure faith, pure intent, and pure actions.

For the next 18 months, amidst the trial, difficulty, and even rejection, I saw her serve with unconditional love, unquestioned integrity, and an unconquerable work ethic.

Initially, Taloa was quiet, but she was not timid; her words had gravity and power. With time and familiarity, she became compassionately bold. All who came in contact with her grew to love, respect, and trust her.

It's interesting to note that a number of ancient societies, like the Greek and Roman Empires, had a tradition of honoring their heroes and esteemed citizens by erecting statues of them in areas of public gathering. They believed that as they looked upon them, they would take upon them some of the qualities that made their champions great. If we followed that tradition today, it would not surprise me to see a likeness of Taloa Solitua Walters in my town square. This book will hopefully serve a similar purpose as we liken her very personal experiences and observations to our own lives.

Captain Moroni, an ancient military leader and prophet of Book of Mormon fame, was honored as a mighty man of God, whose faith and love blessed his people. It was recorded of him that, "If all men had been, and were, and ever would be, like unto Moroni, behold the very powers of Hell would have been shaken forever..." (Alma 48:17). I will go so far as to say that if all people were like unto Taloa Solitua Walters, this world would be a much better place.

If there is one word to describe this woman, it is valiant. I've always wondered what made her "tick," now you and I get to enjoy her revealing the answer.

Stephen L. Weston
Past President Australia Adelaide Mission

Testimonials

As a student of personal progress in my whole lifetime, Spirit Freedom is a breath of fresh air with personal experiences and how to make good choices that can lead to amazing blessings when we understand our purpose in life. Taloa Walters is true 'Genuine Gold' – as an alumna of BYU-Hawaii and a true friend.

Bobby Akoi
Former Brigham Young University Hawaii Bishop

There is a light that seems to bounce off every page and into your heart. I have watched this personal journey unfold, and no matter what the hardship (and there have been so many) grace has filled her heart!

Taloa, my piano teacher, inspiration and true friend, the learning has not been for naught, thank you for allowing us into the pages of your purpose-filled life.

So much wisdom and practical advice to transform our pain into 'R.a.e.s' of love and gratitude.

Cassile Ortega

Taloa invites you into her heart on her spiritual journey of growth and asks you to do the same. Her message is thought-provoking, powerful and deeply personal. This book is a beautiful discovery of how the knowledge of your divine origins can heal your past and guide your future. Taloa communicates that Heavenly Father understands His children better than anyone, and with that understanding, Heavenly Father promises to shape you into the person you were meant to become. In this book, Taloa asks questions that will beg you to search your soul. She will then offer tools to guide you on a path to self-betterment using the teachings of Jesus Christ.

Amy Davis

Taloa Walters

Very humbling and insightful view into the writer's spiritual journey, tasking an array of tools to lead the reader toward their own spiritual freedom.

Tuputala and Melanie Solitua

Testimonials	v
Introduction	xi
Chapter 1: Awaken	1
Chapter 2: Potential	15
Chapter 3: Choice	29
Chapter 4: Power	35
Chapter 5: Connect	45
Chapter 6: Grateful	61
Chapter 7: Vision	73
Chapter 8: Discover	85
Chapter 9: Reflect	93
Chapter 10: Endure	101
Chapter 11: Voice	109
Chapter 12: Inspire	115
Summary & Testimony	121
More Testimonials	123
References	127
Appendices: Affirmations & Essentials Oils (Self Help And Healing)	133
Afterword	141
Acknowledgements	143
About the Author	145

Introduction

Spirit Freedom is intended for this generation and the next, a guide to spiritually prepare for the future. There is so much uncertainty in times ahead yet through the experiences and stories within Spirit Freedom, you may feel peace, hope, love, strength and assurance that difficult times will pass and that through the actual process of change, you will realise the growth and development within yourself, be guided on a distinct path to journey and discover endless potential for happiness that continues beyond this life and into the eternities.

I wrote Spirit Freedom to share my story with the world, with the hope that the lessons I've learned may be a guide, help, positive influence and further understanding of their spiritual journey or path in life. It is my hope that the reader will gain a better understanding and guidance of the process in receiving personal revelation from our Heavenly Father who loves them very much, in order to discover their individual purpose, mission, journey or path in life returning to their heavenly home.

During this COVID-19 period, I am more inspired to share my story with the world with the intention that all have hope for the future, feel their Heavenly Father's love just as I have throughout my life and continue to feel now, and to spiritually prepare for the future.

CHAPTER 1

For each of us, life is a journey.

Heavenly Father designed it for us out of love.

Each of us has unique experiences and characteristics, but

our journey began in the same place before we were

born into this world.

-Henry B. Eyring

The decision that saved my life was a desperate plea for help! This book represents my spiritual journey and how I have achieved Spirit Freedom. You may ask, "What does it mean to have SPIRT FREEDOM?" To answer that question, you need to have an understanding of what a spirit is. Did you know that you are a spirit or intelligence residing in your physical body? It is what makes you,

YOU! Your unique personality, interests, talents, gifts, emotions, and energy in culmination are the essence of your spirit! You existed as a spirit living in a realm of existence awaiting your turn to be born to this world (Pearl of Great Price, 2013, Abraham 3:22-25). Every single human being on this earth has a spirit. Your spirit gives your body life much like electricity channelling through wires to power equipment, tools or appliances. Your spirit gives your body power and energy to function effectively!

Spirit Freedom is the journey of understanding your individual spirit, where you come from, ultimately your purpose on this planet and what happens to you after death! Have you ever asked yourself these questions, "Where am I from?" "What's my purpose in life?" and "What will happen after I die?" These were the questions I asked myself, and I'm grateful to have discovered the answers. Writing this book is my way of sharing these discoveries and inspiring you to discover these answers for yourself too.

Every human being born to this world experiences a uniquely, patterned, and specifically designed life created for the purpose of returning to our heavenly home. Our spiritual journey began long before our birth. We decided and accepted these individual pathways as spirits knowing full well the challenges that we would face. We agreed and promised our heavenly parents that we would conquer all things and return to them some day. We also knew that any choice we would make in life could impact, affect or alter those pathways. The choice each individual person makes absolutely determines the outcomes, leading to their progression or regression, development or stagnation and ultimately achieving their potential or unrealised ability. Why don't we remember making these promises to return to our heavenly home? Well, for everyone, there is a veil of forgetfulness that we pass through at birth where we would gradually forget our heavenly home and truly begin our earthly stage of progression to rediscover our journey home. If we remembered all that happened before birth, then it wouldn't really be a test of agency for us. Knowing all the answers would be like cheating in a test, and we would not truly learn, grow and discover our path back to our heavenly home.

Awaken

I want to foremost thank you for joining me as I share my spiritual journey with you. I hope that my journey will inspire, motivate and encourage you on your spiritual journey in attaining Spirit Freedom and ultimately understand the concepts of Faith, Hope and Peace in order to return to our heavenly parents and heavenly home!

Two lessons I learned as a child was, firstly, that the only way to go when you hit rock bottom is up and secondly, with our Heavenly Father's help I can overcome fear, guilt, despair, anxiety, depression, negative thoughts and emotions. With His help, I can believe that all things I want to accomplish or achieve in this life are possible!!!

My parents are faithful members of The Church of Jesus Christ of Latter Day Saints and exemplary in their love for our Heavenly Father and Jesus Christ, which they extended to everyone. I love my parents dearly, and I am so grateful for their guidance, teachings and examples of faith in our Heavenly Father and Jesus Christ. Growing up, I attended church with my siblings every Sunday and learned about our Heavenly Father, Jesus Christ and the Holy Ghost (members of the Godhead), particularly their roles in our lives, and about the Plan of Happiness (more details in the next chapter). This knowledge ultimately came to my rescue in my time of need.

Being raised in the Gospel gave me comfort and a foundation of faith and belief but true understanding of the concepts of Faith, Hope and Peace began at seven years old. I discovered that developing an understanding of these concepts in my childhood essentially provided spiritual enlightenment, inner strength and empowerment, opening the door to ultimate potential and success throughout my life.

Although my parents did their very best to protect their children, at the age of five, I was molested by a distant relative in our home. I felt violated, disgusted, unworthy and guilty. I kept this secret from my family for the next two years because I was embarrassed and ashamed. I suffered silently, hiding feelings of shame, guilt, disgust and despair. I kept up the pretence by appearing happy, content, and normal; doing everything that was expected of me, yet deep down I was sad, miserable and unhappy. I made every effort to try to forget what happened to me and searched for ways to overcome these negative feelings. I thought that giving my best in school, church, and home would make me feel better about myself! It seemed the harder I tried to do what was right the worse I felt because I was dishonest in keeping this secret and blamed myself for everything! I started to feel that I was a burden to my family. Bearing the weight of the secret on my shoulders over the next two years eventually took a toll on my state of mind. I found myself hitting rock bottom, and the feelings of hopelessness, unworthiness and darkness were too much to bear. There was no escape from the sadness, and I decided that ending my life was the best thing for everyone. I was seven years old at this time. Alone in the bathroom and just before attempting to end my life, a thought instantly crossed my mind to "pray for help"! In that desperate moment, I mustered up every bit of faith and prayed with all my mind, heart and spirit, in complete surrender to Heavenly Father for help!

Immediately after I had thought the words, "Heavenly Father, please help me!" I physically felt arms embrace me, holding and giving me the most incredible hug. I felt pure love, and light which seemed to fill my whole body, from my head to my feet. It was a feeling that I'd never felt before, yet a familiar feeling of being home in our Heavenly Father's arms! After that, peace came over me, and I knew I mattered to our Heavenly Father and that He loved me and answered my plea for help. An image of Jesus Christ filled my mind, and I felt all the negative feelings and thoughts I previously felt wiped away. I was filled with enormous gratitude and immense hope for the first time in two years!

Everything that I was taught in Church from that moment on had new meaning to me and my perspective on life and everything I had ever learned before completely changed. I had been 'awakened' to the divine love I felt in our Heavenly Father's arms before birth and truly continued my spiritual journey home to our heavenly parents and heavenly home. Everything I had learned from my parents and teachers in church finally made sense!

The magnitude of that experience brought a deeper understanding of the concepts of Faith, Hope, and Peace; the crucial pillars of joy and happiness in this life and eternal life, after this stage of progression and development. I desired to do all I could to feel that same embrace I felt from our Heavenly Father each day of my life! I drew strength from that experience, and it became the source of motivation for me in all areas of learning because I understood my worth! I knew with all my heart that our Heavenly Father and Jesus Christ's love for me was real and true!

Did you know that according to the World Health Organization, child abuse, molestation and sexual abuse is a global dilemma? Did you know that "3 in 4 children experienced physical, sexual or violence abuse worldwide in 2019?" This is disturbing because its effects are devastating! Furthermore, child sexual abuse is connected to later emotional and behavioural problems in victims and toward alcoholism, depression, mental illness and suicide. (World Health Organization, 2020). A study in 2007 in Queensland alone shows that 70% of psychiatric patients were sexually abused as children, while another case in 2012 carried out in 27 prisons in NSW found 65% males and females were sexually and physically abused as children. In addition, between 2017 and 2019, approximately 145,426 children and adolescents were sexually abused or assaulted.

With growing numbers in cases of sexually, physically, emotionally and verbally abused victims, this quote by Richard G. Scott, one of my favourite individuals who I met later in life, said,

> *"Healing best begins with your sincere prayer asking your Father in Heaven for help. That use of your agency allows divine intervention. When you permit it, the love of the Savior will soften your heart and break the cycle of abuse that can transform a victim into an aggressor. Adversity, even when caused willfully by others' unrestrained appetite, can be a source of growth when viewed from the perspective of eternal principle." (Doctrine &Covenants 122:7) (Scott, R. G., 1992)*

I know with all my heart that our Heavenly Father will help you just as He has helped me. My plea for help opened the door to a miracle, leading to further direction and guidance in my life! This process I've coined as "R.A.E." has aided me to progress and develop faith gradually over the following years.

These following steps are:
1. 'R' represents recognising and acknowledging that we all need help, complete surrender or humility to our Heavenly Father's will allows spiritual intervention, revelation and inspiration. "We need divine help to conquer all things in life" (King James Version of the Holy Bible, Proverbs 3: 5-7, King Solomon of Israel, Approx. 970-937 BCE)
2. 'A' represents asking Heavenly Father for help with all our mind, might, strength, heart and spirit. (King James Version. Bible, 2013. Matthew 7:7-8, Apostle Matthew, approx. 70 AD)
3. 'E' represents embracing the answers by listening, feeling and doing what's required or necessary to progress, grow and return to our heavenly home! Embracing our Heavenly Father's answers in order to choose a different path to take! (Book of Mormon, 3 Nephi 12:20, Jesus Christ's visit to the inhabitants of Ancient America, 34AD)

Daily efforts of positive actions can help you access power and strength, building on each spiritual experience you have! This is Spirit Freedom! Have patience and remember that it is a gradual process and does not always happen overnight. Continuously develop a positive mindset each day by applying R.A.E.

Instantly applying R.A.E helped me remember that divine love I experienced before birth and impacted the decisions I made as a child, has led to many other wonderful experiences in my life and moulded the person I am today!

Faith, Hope and Peace are the pillars for spiritual growth, knowledge, insight, personal development, eternal joy and happiness no matter where you are spiritually right now.

Faith

Faith is the foundation of things hoped for and evidence or proof of things not seen (King James Version, Hebrews 11:1). Furthermore, faith is not to have a perfect knowledge of things; if you have faith then you hope for things which are not seen, but are true (Book of Mormon, Alma 32:21). To have faith is to have confidence in something or someone. Faith in Jesus Christ is the foundation of eternal salvation and happiness. Faith is a principle of action and power to command elements; heal the sick or impact any amount of situations when required (Book of Mormon, Jacob 4:4-7). Most importantly, through faith you can receive a remission of your sins and eventually stand in the presence of our Heavenly Father one day!

Hope

Hope is a feeling of belief and a plea for a specific thing to materialise. It is also a person or thing that may help or save someone. Having 'Hope in Christ' is to believe in everything written in the scriptures about Him and His Atoning sacrifice. Our hope is that Jesus Christ will through His grace and mercy make up the difference after our best efforts in life in order for us to stand sinless or spotless in the presence of our Heavenly Father (King James Version, Romans 15:4; Book of Mormon, 2 Nephi 31:20).

Peace

Peace is liberty from disorder; experiencing tranquillity, emotional and mental calmness of mind. Jesus Christ is the Prince of Peace and it is through him that we can have spiritual peace and assurance that as we do our part and become the best version of ourselves than all will work out in the end no matter what is happening in the world around us (King James Version, Isaiah 9:6 -around 800BCE; Book of Mormon, 2 Nephi 19:6-around 550BCE).

Commitment to understanding and exercising these concepts will lead you to achieve Spirit Freedom, spiritually preparing to deal with a future that is uncertain. In your efforts of applying these concepts, you can change your circumstances whatever they may be. These concepts will help you develop a mindset of abundance and open your life to unlimited potential and opportunities. At the end of this chapter, I will outline some simple strategies that may improve personal results, will give deeper insights into your incredible spirit, worth, abilities, and potential! You will also discover how these concepts will expand your awareness of the beauty of life, changing your outlook and perspective on life!

Early Childhood Education and Care (ECEC) is one of my passions because I believe that spiritual development is paramount in optimal child development. I truly believe that as parents and teachers incorporate spiritual development within their homes and educational environments by teaching children concepts of Faith, Hope and Peace, children will thrive in all other essential developmental areas such as physical, cognitive, linguistic, social and emotional. Through Spiritual development, children will hone into understanding their individual spirits and access power to live the lives they are meant to live, excelling and succeeding in all areas of life! Providing opportunities for our children to receive spiritual development will help them know that they could turn to Heavenly Father for help to overcome life's challenges, negative influences, impacts, or emotional effects of physical, emotional, sexual or verbal abuse. Helping children to recognise the influence of the Holy Ghost will help them feel peace, assurance, increased belief and guidance to overcome all negative things and achieve Spirit Freedom early in life! Can you imagine the impact on each child when they understand their vision and purpose in life? They will spiritually be prepared to conquer the storms, whirlwinds and challenges of life. Children will be equipped with the understanding that with their Heavenly Father's help, they can achieve success and freedom in all areas of life!

Tuputala & Siaunofo
(my parents)

Nana Tina
(my grandmother)

Besides my parents, an incredible influence in my life growing up was my grandmother, Lelefua Tusa or Tina (nickname). I loved her very dearly and remember reading the Samoan Bible with her at the dining table each day. She passed away in 1994, but her example of reading scriptures (Bible) will stay with me forever! Studying the scriptures (Bible, Book of Mormon, Doctrine and Covenants, Pearl of Great Price, other church literature etc.) became my personal connection to understanding the tremendous love our Heavenly Father, Jesus Christ and the Holy Ghost have for us. It helped me to understand more about the Godhead, Jesus Christ's Atonement for all mankind, and our role in the Plan of Happiness.

One of the most significant practices in our home was personal and family prayers. I had received my own personal witness that prayer did work! James, a devoted disciple of Jesus Christ in the Holy Bible, expresses that,

> *"If any of you lack wisdom let him ask of God, that giveth to all men liberally, and upbraideth not; and it shall be given him." (King James Version, James 1:5)*

I discovered that our Heavenly Father exists, is real, loves me and answers prayers!!! This truth of exercising Faith by asking for help when we need it allows heavenly assistance and can reaffirm our Heavenly Father's existence each day! I applied this when going to school, learning the English language, overcoming the effects of bullying, discrimination, prejudices and many other challenges in life. I learned that seeking Heavenly Father's help to overcome any problem or challenge not only helped me personally, but I began to recognise a pattern of heavenly assistance evident in the lives of thousands of people in history, not only in the scriptures from applying the concept of Faith through prayer and asking Heavenly Father for help. Many stories in the Bible were individuals who applied concepts of Faith, Hope and Peace!

Another favourite scripture found in the Bible, Luke, says:

"For with God nothing shall be impossible." (King James Version, Luke 1:37)

This powerful verse of scripture is a great truth that I've known since the night I felt our Heavenly Father's loving arms around me! I believed I could overcome any obstacle, achieve any goal I set for myself and accomplish any dream with His help in my life! That was all I needed to believe to conquer life's challenges! Prayer and scripture study was my way to hold onto the love I felt from our Heavenly Father. My faith began to grow, and hope became a daily feeling as I thought about Jesus Christ and the suffering He went through for me. I finally understood what gave me hope and peace that night. It was Jesus Christ's atoning sacrifice that wiped away the guilt, unworthiness, and embarrassment. The peace I felt was the power of the Holy Ghost, and at that moment, I understood how the Godhead work together to benefit all of our Heavenly Father's spirit children in this life! I understood why the Plan of Happiness is so important and how it culminates the incomprehensible love of the Godhead; Our Heavenly Father, Jesus Christ and the Holy Ghost, who are separate beings but one in purpose. Jesus Christ who is the author of the Plan of Happiness, cleansing us through the Atonement (shedding of his blood on the cross, and suffering in Gethsemane; where he bled from every pore and taking upon him everyone's sins), the ultimate sacrifice that allows us to have hope. Through the power of the Holy Ghost we feel peace, happiness, joy and other feelings described in Galatians 5:22-23,

> **22** *But the fruit of the Spirit is love, joy, peace, longsuffering, gentleness, goodness, faith,*
> **23** *Meekness, temperance: against such there is no law. (King James Version, Galatians 4:22-23)*

I feel peace when listening to the modern-day prophets Heavenly Father has called since the restoration of The Church of Jesus Christ of Latter Day Saints and everything they would say. I came to understand that the Holy Ghost reveals truth through the feelings listed above, of love, joy, peace, longsuffering, gentleness, goodness, faith, meekness, and temperance (King James Version, John 14:26). The Holy Ghost is my spiritual guide and compass to knowing that I am on the right track returning to my heavenly home. These powerful feelings also guided me to knowing and recognising whether I was in the right places, watching appropriate media, listening to truths and reading personal development literature.

I love this verse in the Holy Bible, John shares with us in chapter 3:16,

> **16** *For God so loved the world, that he gave his only begotten Son, that whosoever believeth in him should not perish, but have everlasting life. (King James Version, John 3:16)*

I discovered that by following Jesus Christ's example and taking advantage of His atoning sacrifice for us, through repentance, and through the power of the Holy Ghost, I would continue to feel our Heavenly Father's love for me each day!

People may be sceptical and say that the solution seems too simple and cliché but going through the experience as a child, experiencing adverse negativity, darkness, depression, spiritual and emotional anguish and pain, guilt, unworthiness, and feeling a burden to my family was far from simple and all too real! Yet through a desperate and sincere plea to God, our Heavenly Father for help, I found love, hope, and peace. Many times, the solution is simple; prayer is simple, but we sometimes get in our own way, or overthink things, and sometimes make life more difficult and complicated than it really is.

If you're wondering why I asked God and not my parents for help, as I mentioned earlier, in my seven-year-old mindset, I felt no one could help me at the time or help me through this. For me, it was my last resort, and it was the choice I made that brought about my miracle.

No one needs to go through what I went through to find God, but if you're ever feeling how I felt, you can definitely ask our Heavenly Father for help. I know if you truly ask Him with all your mind, heart and spirit, He will answer your prayers, as he did for me. I know he loves all His spirit children, those living in this world right now, everyone who has ever lived and passed into the Spirit World and everyone yet to be born (more details on this topic in the next chapter).

The following four activities helped me each day and may help you in developing a positive mindset:

1. Using positive words, thoughts, and experiences to replace negative words, thoughts or experiences daily (strategies also used in Neurological Linguistic Programming)
2. Daily communication with our Heavenly Father through prayer, expressing gratitude and requesting assistance in anything you may need! (Meditation techniques, manifestations, law of attraction, and vision boards)
3. Connecting to your spirit to understand your interests, talents, gifts and purpose. (Personal development, self-help literature, self-healing strategies used in Reiki, Applied Kinesiology, health and wellness regiments, self-care routine and practices)
4. Connecting to others through expression (music, literature, art, sport, social media, talents, gifts, etc.).

I will be discussing many of these topics and sharing knowledge on these areas throughout my book.

Here are some strategies to begin your spiritual journey to Spirit Freedom!

1. **Daily Prayer:** No matter what you're going through, remember to sincerely pray to our Heavenly Father for guidance, strength and assistance each morning, throughout the day and night! Make it part of your daily routine! If you've never prayed before here is a guide to follow:
   - Our Heavenly Father/Our Father in Heaven
   - I thank thee……(express what you're grateful for)
   - I ask thee…..(express what you're in need of)
   - In the name of Jesus Christ, Amen (ends our prayer because Christ is the way, the truth and the light back to our Heavenly Father).

2. **Personal Revelation:** Take a few minutes to truly listen to the answers that will always come through positive, uplifting, and inspirational feelings and thoughts connected to love, hope, light, peace, joy, assurance and comfort. Be aware that the answers may not always come straight away but could come through other people, events throughout the day or signs that only you may understand.

3. **Daily expression:** Act on the positive thoughts, ideas and feelings that come to you. Healing requires effort on your part. Seek to daily do good deeds, uplifting service, and choose to be happy! Do what makes you happy and feel love. Trust this! The effort you put in every day will lift your spirit, increase your confidence, and you will truly find yourself and connect to other people on that same journey, to Spirit Freedom.

Taloa Walters

The pure love and light that filled my whole body was confirmation from a Loving Heavenly Father that I matter to Him. The knowledge that Heavenly Father loves all His spirit children and that the tender mercies of our Saviour, Jesus Christ can bring healing, hope, peace, joy and guidance....I was spiritually 'awakened' to heavenly love and continued my spiritual journey home, to my heavenly home!

-Taloa Walters

CHAPTER 2

God's great plan of

HAPPINESS

enables us to be transformed.

-Dallin H. Oaks

We all have incredible potential beyond what we can imagine. Have you ever asked yourself these questions, "What is this Plan of Happiness?" or "Why is this Plan of Happiness important?" or "What's my purpose on earth?" or "Where do our spirits go after death?" Did you know that the answers to all those questions are found in the scriptures?

Another passion of mine is researching the Gospel or The Church of Jesus Christ of Latter Day Saints by reading all scriptures or the word of God available to me. This includes the Holy Bible, the Book of Mormon, the Doctrine and Covenants and the Pearl of Great

Price, as well as other church literature revealing truth regarding the Plan of Happiness. I believe that Heavenly Father loves us so much that he provided the path back to Him. He has preserved the Bible which is the record of His dealings with the Tribe of Judah, one of the 12 tribes of Israel or Jacob, a covenant Heavenly Father made with Jacob's grandfather, Abraham. The Book of Mormon is a record of the descendants of the Tribe of Joseph sold by his brothers into Egypt and their dealings with Heavenly Father, translated by the power of God and published in 1830 in New York. The Doctrine and Covenants is a record of the revelations regarding the Restoration of The Church of Jesus Christ of Latter Days Saints in this dispensation of time through the Prophet Joseph Smith. The Pearl of Great Price includes the modern translation of the books of Moses through the power of God to the prophet Joseph Smith, also including a record of Abraham's writings from Egyptian scrolls. The Pearl of Great Price also includes the Articles of Faith of The Church of Jesus Christ of Latter Day Saints explaining the church's beliefs and values, Joseph Smith Translation of the Book of Matthew according to the Lord's command and Joseph Smith History.

From the scriptures, I learned that Jesus Christ set the perfect example for us to follow and everything he did is for our benefit (King James Version, John 14:6). I understood that the picture of Jesus Christ that filled my mind and the peace that came over me when all the negative emotions and feelings were gone was the cleansing power of Jesus Christ's Atonement for me at seven years of age. I felt hope and gratitude for what Jesus Christ did for me, and I believed that by striving to be better I could contribute to alleviating the pain Jesus Christ suffered in Gethsemane; that took place so many years ago for everyone's sins, mistakes, sorrows and pains (King James Version, John 15:13). I am so grateful for all scriptures because we need all of them to see the bigger picture of the eternal Plan of Happiness, the pathway to returning to our heavenly home. I would spend hours researching answers to many of my questions! I couldn't get enough knowledge, and there was so much to learn, so many questions to find answers to! Why couldn't Jesus Christ have visited other nations of the world to teach them the same things He taught people in Jerusalem? If he did visit other nations, then it would make sense to keep an open mind to other scriptures or records that exist too? I found the Holy Bible, the Book of Mormon, the Doctrine and Covenants and the Pearl of Great Price contained all the answers to all my questions! As I continued to study the Eternal Plan of Happiness, the Holy Ghost revealed truths to my spirit through feelings of love, hope and peace.

As mentioned in chapter one, 'Awaken' we all existed as intelligences or spirits, and we agreed to accept and follow this plan knowing that it would lead us back home to our Heavenly parents. Discovering and living this Eternal Plan of Happiness has brought joy and happiness to my life! As you come to understand and know that this Eternal Plan of Happiness is true, it will affect the way you live your life, and you will come to realise that this Plan of Happiness is a wonderful gift!

Did you know that approximately 2% of the 7.9 billion people of the world's population possess knowledge about this Eternal Plan of Happiness only because they have sought after it? The rest of the population have not yet discovered it or even know that it exists, mainly because they have not sought knowledge about it! (LDS, 2020).

How could I share this knowledge with all my spirit brothers and sisters throughout the whole world? I remember setting a goal to become a missionary for The Church of Jesus Christ of Latter Day Saints and share the love, hope and peace I felt from living the Eternal Plan of Happiness! The fact that every spirit was present in that heavenly council and accepted this Eternal Plan of Happiness before we were all born to this earth was refreshing, hopeful and amazing to me! (Pearl of Great Price, Abraham 3:22-26). Why don't we remember any of this? The veil of forgetfulness took any memory of that away from us so that through our agency, we have the choice to return to our heavenly home!

I felt the power of the Holy Ghost through feelings of joy and peace when listening to church leaders and knew that they were chosen by our Heavenly Father to lead us all back to our heavenly home. Everything made more sense to me, and I felt the love of our Heavenly Father and Jesus Christ stronger as I read the scriptures. I felt excited listening to the words of prophets, apostles, church leaders, and teachers, including my parents, especially when it was about the Plan of Happiness. Over the next couple of years, reading and studying the words of the Holy Bible, Book of Mormon, Pearl of Great Price, the Doctrine and Covenants and other books written on this subject was a huge priority to me! I absorbed everything I could get my hands on to read about the subject. The words of Matthew came to mind,

"But seek ye first the kingdom of God, and his righteousness; and all these things shall be added unto you." (King James Version, Matthew 6:33)

My love and gratitude towards Heavenly Father and Jesus Christ grew as I continued to study his purpose for me. The words of the Prophet Joseph Smith in regards to the Plan of Salvation, Redemption and Happiness motivated more learning and study of the subject for me. Joseph Smith said,

"At the first organization in heaven we were all present and saw the Savior chosen and appointed, and the plan of salvation made and we sanctioned it." (Smith, J., 2011)

Without the knowledge of this Eternal Plan of Happiness, all would be lost. It is crucial for everyone to realise their individual purpose and ultimate potential; otherwise they could be lost not only in this life but the next state of existence after death.

'Potential' reveals my search and pursuit of knowledge regarding the Eternal Plan of Happiness, which led to more understanding of who I am and where I fit into this Eternal Plan! As Heavenly Father's spirit children, we can inherit all that He has and possesses including eternal happiness and joy when we return to His presence!

I remember looking forward to my baptism, as it was customary in The Church of Jesus Christ of Latter Day Saints that children were to be taught the gospel in preparation for their baptism by their eighth birthday. I loved reading and studying talks, speeches and other books that lifted my spirit. I felt the power of love from my Heavenly Father and Jesus Christ through the Holy Ghost regularly each day as my gospel studies became a priority.

In the Doctrine and Covenants section 68 verses 25, modern day revelation through the Prophet Joseph Smith read,

> *25 And again, inasmuch as parents have children in Zion, or in any of her stakes which are organized, that teach them not to understand the doctrine of repentance, faith in Christ the Son of the living God, and of baptism and the gift of the Holy Ghost by the laying on of the hands, then eight years old, the sin be upon the heads of the parents. (Doctrine and Covenants, Section 68:25)*

I remember being quite serious about my preparation, and I wanted to fully understand my commitment and covenants before my baptism. The covenants I read about in the Book of Mormon, Mosiah chapter 18 verse 8-10 read,

> *8 And it came to pass that he said unto them: Behold, here are the waters of Mormon (for thus were they called) and now, as ye are desirous to come into the of God, and to be called his people, and are willing to bear one another's burdens, that they may be light;*
> *9 Yea, and are willing to mourn with those that mourn; yea, and comfort those that stand in need of comfort, and to stand as witnesses of God at all times and in all things, and in all places that ye may be in, even until death, that ye may be redeemed of God, and be numbered with those of the first resurrection, that ye may have eternal life—*
> *10 Now I say unto you, if this be the desire of your hearts, what have you against being baptized in the name of the Lord, as a witness before him that ye have entered into a covenant with him, that ye will serve him and keep his commandments that he may pour out his Spirit more abundantly upon you? (Book of Mormon, Mosiah 18:8-10)*

I was so excited for my baptism because I knew that by accepting the gospel and following Jesus Christ's example of baptism, I would be forgiven of all my sins, and officially begin my journey as his disciple. Through baptism, I would be entering into His kingdom on earth, choosing to belong to His Church that held the priesthood authority from Him. I knew that this same authority was given to His prophets, passed down through priesthood linage to my father, giving him the authority to baptise me. I remember reading about Christ's baptism in Matthew chapter 3 verses 13 to 17,

> *13 Then cometh Jesus from Galilee to Jordan unto John, to be baptized of him.*
> *14 But John forbad him, saying, I have need to be baptized of thee, and comest thou to me?*
> *15 And Jesus answering said unto him, Suffer it to be so now: for thus it becometh to fulfill all righteousness. Then he suffered him.*
> *16 And Jesus, when he was baptized, went up straightway out of the water: and, lo, the heavens were opened unto him, and he saw the Spirit of God descending like a dove, and lighting upon him.*
> *17 And lo a voice from heaven, saying, This is my beloved, in whom I am well pleased. (King James Version, Matthew 3:13-17)*

I knew that Jesus Christ was perfect but being baptised was showing us the way so that we could follow Him. Later Christ shares the importance of baptism by the authority from Him, in the *book of John*, he states,

> *5 Jesus answered, Verily, verily, I say unto thee, Except a man be born of water and of the Spirit, he cannot enter into the kingdom of God. (King James Version, John 3:5)*

I knew that this was the path to follow, and as the day drew closer, I grew more excited and desired to spiritually prepare as much as I could. Along with preparing for my baptism, during this time my grandmother lived with us and being the oldest girl in my family,

Potential

I accompanied her to other church denominations as she was not a member of The Church of Jesus Christ of Latter Day Saints. Even in her 60s, she was searching for truth. I remember each Sunday going to several different Christian denominations with her; the Presbyterian, Baptist, Tongan church, LMS, etc. I listened to everything that was taught within these congregations. I learned quite young that most of them taught similar teachings about Jesus Christ and I'm reminded of what Brigham Young, the second prophet of this dispensation of The Church of Jesus Christ of Latter Day Saints said,

> *"We, the Latter-day Saints, take the liberty of believing more than our Christian brethren: we not only believe . . . the Bible, but . . . the whole of the plan of salvation that Jesus has given to us. Do we differ from others who believe in the Lord Jesus Christ? No, only in believing more."*
> *(Millet, R. L., 2001)*

I found that although most of the Christian church denominations I visited with my grandmother taught what was in the Holy Bible, I understood why there was a need for modern revelation and additional scriptures from our loving Heavenly Father for clarity in regards to His Eternal Plan of Happiness. My personal readings, research and study of the scriptures lead me to the basic understanding of the overall Eternal Plan of Happiness, in the following diagram.

The following are a few references from my personal research to explain the above Eternal Plan of Happiness. The numbers cross-reference to the numbered titles in the diagram.

1. Pre-Mortal Life - John 17:5 (Lived in the presence of God before the world was created); John 17:26 (Heavenly Father loves Jesus Christ and all His spirit children) Pearl of Great Price, Moses 1:39 (Purpose of God for all His spirit children) Moses 3:7 (everything was created spiritually before their physical natural form) Moses 4: 1-4 (Plans were presented. Christ and Lucifer, Heavenly Father chose Christ's plan and Lucifer was cast out becoming Satan) Pearl of Great Price,

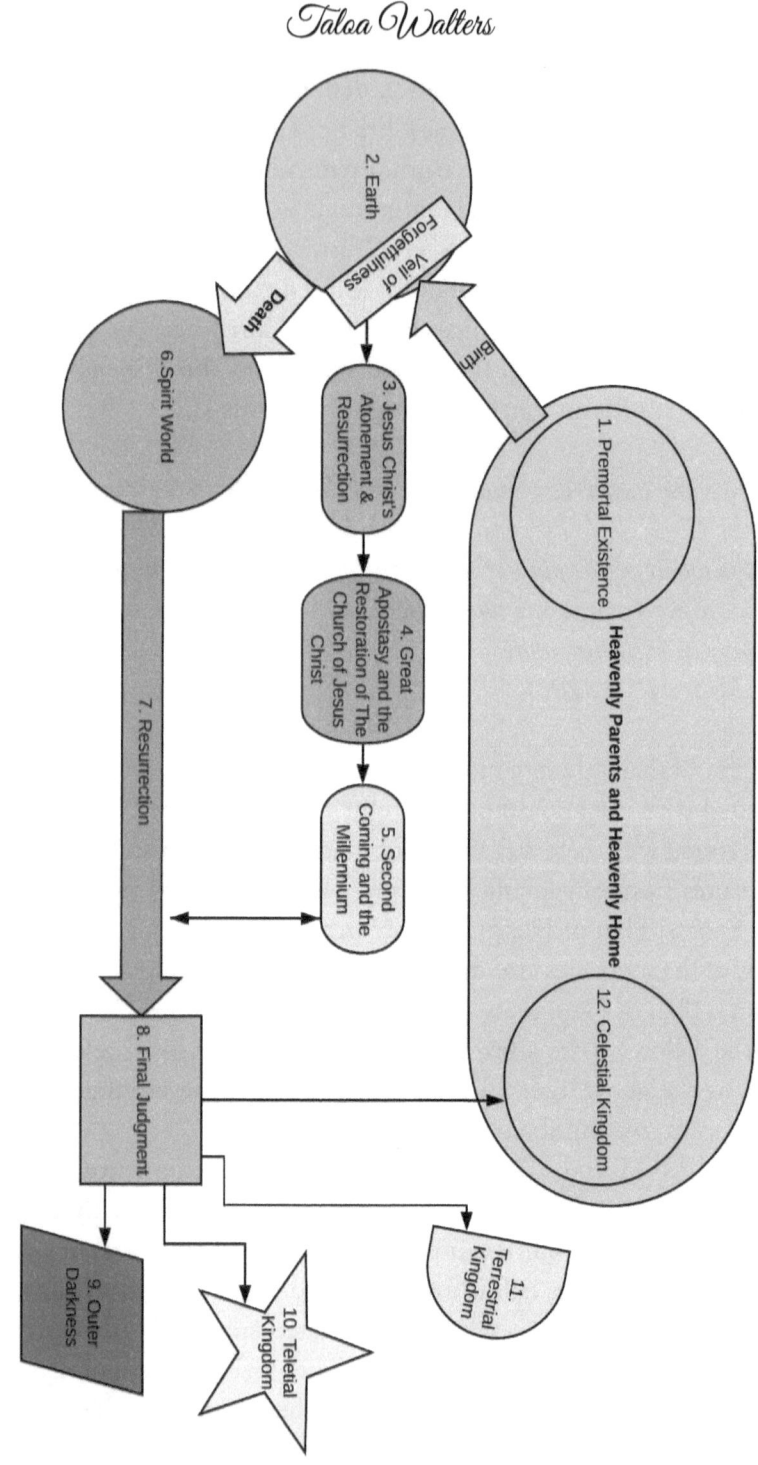

22

Potential

Abraham 3:22-28 (Abraham was shown the pre-mortal life and that we were all present in the council of heaven before the creation of all things, plans were presented, and we chose who we would follow).
https://www.churchofjesuschrist.org/study/new-era/2015/02/what-we-know-about-premortal-life?lang=eng

2. Mortal life on Earth – Genesis 1:26-27 (All people were created in the image of our Heavenly Father) 1 Corinthians 6:19-20 (Your body is a temple) Old Testament, Joshua 24:15; Book of Mormon, Alma 34:32-34, 2 Nephi 2:27; New Testament, John 17:3 (This mortal life is to learn about our Heavenly Father and Jesus Christ, choose to follow, keep the commandments, spiritually develop so that we are prepared to live with them one day).
https://www.churchofjesuschrist.org/study/manual/gospel-topics/mortality?lang=eng

3. Atonement of Jesus Christ – New Testament, John 17:4-5; Book of Mormon, Alma 34:8-9; Doctrine and Covenants 19:2; Pearl of Great Price, Moses 4:2 (Mission of Jesus Christ to sanctify all and reconcile all to our Heavenly Father) Old Testament, Isaiah 53:3-5 (Christ suffered for all our sins, pains and sorrow) New Testament, Matthew 11:28-30 (Come unto Christ and he will ease your burdens giving you rest).
https://www.churchofjesuschrist.org/study/manual/gospel-topics/atonement-of-jesus-christ?lang=eng

4. Apostasy and Restoration – 2 Thessalonians 2:1-3 (Great apostasy prophesied by Paul before the Second coming of the Lord, Jesus Christ) New Testament, Acts 3:21, Ephesian 1:10, Revelations 14:6 (Restoration of the Gospel of Jesus Christ will prepare all people for the Second coming of Jesus Christ).
https://www.churchofjesuschrist.org/study/manual/gospel-topics/atonement-of-jesus-christ?lang=eng

5. Second Coming of Jesus Christ and the Millennium – King James Version, Old Testament, Job 19:25, Isaiah 40:11; King James Version, New Testament, Matthew 16:27, Revelations 1:7; Book of Mormon, 3 Nephi 27:16; Doctrine and Covenants 27:16; Pearl of Great Price, Articles of Faith 10 (Jesus Christ will ascend from Heaven in glory at His Second Coming and will reign on the earth forever).
https://www.churchofjesuschrist.org/study/manual/teachings-joseph-smith/chapter-21?lang=eng

6. Spirit World – New Testament, 1 Peter 3:19, 4:6; Book of Mormon, Ether 3:16, Alma 34:34; Doctrine and Covenants 138, 138:30 (A realm where spirits reside after death, divided into prison and paradise. Christ visited the spirit prison and the gospel is taught to those in spirit prison who had not had the opportunity to learn about The Church of Jesus Christ in mortality).
https://www.churchofjesuschrist.org/study/manual/gospel-topics/spirit-world?lang=eng

7. Resurrection – New Testament, 1 Corinthians 15:20-22 (Because of Christ all will be resurrected, after death there will be a time when your immortal body and spirit will be reunited never to be separated again).
https://www.churchofjesuschrist.org/study/manual/gospel-topics/resurrection?lang=eng

8. Final Judgment – New Testament, Revelations 20:12 (After the Second coming of Christ and the Millennium all will be judged according to their faith and works during their mortal life).
https://www.churchofjesuschrist.org/study/manual/gospel-principles/chapter-46-the-final-judgment?lang=eng

9. Outer Darkness – New Testament, 2 Peter 2:4; Doctrine and Covenants 29:38; (another word for this is Hell, hell fire which is a place of endless spiritual torment and darkness after the final judgment. Those that reside here are Satan and those that follow Him).
https://www.churchofjesuschrist.org/study/scriptures/gs/outer-darkness?lang=eng

10. Telestial kingdom or Telestial glory – King James Version, New Testament, 1 Corinthians 15:41; Book of Mormon, Mosiah 15:26; Doctrine and Covenants. Section 76:81 (the lowest of the three kingdoms or glory compared to the stars, those spirits resurrected last and worthy for this glory or kingdom. Those that live here were not righteous on earth, did not believe in Jesus Christ and did not keep the commandments).
https://www.churchofjesuschrist.org/study/manual/gospel-topics/telestial-kingdom?lang=eng

11. Terrestrial kingdom or Terrestrial glory – King James Version, New Testament, 1 Corinthians 15:40; Doctrine and Covenants 76:71, 88:38 (this glory or kingdom excels the Telestial glory or Kingdom. This is the middle degree compared to the moon and those that will reside here are righteous people that did not accept Jesus Christ and His gospel in life but accepted it in the spirit world or did not keep all the commandments).
https://www.churchofjesuschrist.org/study/manual/gospel-topics/terrestrial-kingdom?lang=eng

12. Celestial kingdom – King James Version, New Testament, 1 Corinthians 15:40-42; Doctrine and Covenants 76: 68-70, 131:1-4 (This kingdom is compared to the glory of the sun. Those that will preside here are those that have been righteous in life, accepted the Gospel of Jesus and were baptised members of his Church, The Church of Jesus Christ of Latter Day Saints.

They kept all the commandments and obtained all ordinances for exaltation within His Gospel on earth).
https://www.churchofjesuschrist.org/study/manual/gospel-topics/celestial-kingdom?lang=eng

I know that the Plan of Happiness is true, through the power of the Holy Ghost! I know that as you sincerely enquire of our Heavenly Father whether these things are true through prayer that you will receive your answer. It is one of the most important choices you will ever make because it will lead to the path you choose to follow in life. Taking this step will set you on a path that will lead you back to our Heavenly Father's presence. This knowledge was essential for me growing up and helped me to understand my true identity and my relationship with our Heavenly Father and Jesus Christ, which was a pivoting point in my life.

I felt love, hope, peace and joy reading more literature about the Plan of Happiness because it was all part of my healing process and gave me insight to my miracle at seven. The truth about the Eternal Plan of Happiness was revealed to me through the peaceful feelings and understanding I received through the power of the Holy Ghost. It all made complete sense to me!

I was so grateful to have access to the resources I had in The Church of Jesus Christ of Latter Day Saints, not only being raised by faithful parents but all who volunteered to serve in callings (assignments) that I had contact with as a child enlightened my soul. The awareness of things taught to me during those years after my baptism uplifted me and transformed me in mind and spirit. The incredible contrast from the darkness I felt before my miracle to love, light, hope and faith, increased as I continued to study and apply concepts, truths and knowledge, and gradually brought more brightness and light into my life.

In case you're wondering why share it now, to be honest, as a young child and in my youth, I felt these feelings and emotions but could not find the words to explain, express or even understand my miracles. It's taken almost half of a lifetime to learn how to explain my experience, express it and to share how it has blessed my life up to this point in time. I've always wanted to share my story and I feel inspired now more than ever to share it with you. As a young child, feeling that incredible love was an answer to my prayer from our Heavenly Father. I knew how I felt, but because it was so personal to me, I didn't know how to explain it. I couldn't deny that it happened and chose to do everything I could to stay close to that feeling of love from our Heavenly Father.

If you're asking, how does sharing this Eternal Plan of Happiness connect to my childhood experience, well, the more I studied and learned about this plan, the stronger I felt my Heavenly Father's love for me. As I continued to read the scriptures and any other church literature I had access to, I felt that same love, hope, assurance, light, forgiveness, comfort and peace I felt during my miracle when I was a child.

A few suggestions that helped me and I would encourage you to think about and do:

1. Ask yourself, "Is living with our Heavenly Father, Jesus Christ, and my loved ones after this life important to me?" If your answer is YES then knowing whether this "Eternal Plan of Happiness" is important, real and true to you will have a phenomenal impact in your life.
2. Please read the scriptures relating to this Eternal Plan and during that process, pray and listen to the thoughts in your mind and the feelings in your heart to know for yourself if this plan is real and true. You may access the scriptures at https://www.churchofjesuschrist.org/study/scriptures?lang=eng
3. If your thoughts and feelings tell you that these things are true then you can access more information on what to do next at
https://www.comeuntochrist.org/belong/church-community/how-to-become-a-latter-day-saint

The knowledge of the Eternal Plan of Happiness is worth seeking out, learning about, applying its principles and living by its concepts. The consequences that follow will be nothing short of miraculous blessings.

- Taloa Walters

CHAPTER 3

You have agency, and you are free to choose. But there is actually

no free agency. Agency has its price. You have to pay

the consequences of your choices.

-Dieter F. Uchtdorf

In every situation we each have an opportunity to choose goodness, love, hope, peace, joy and happiness. You can also learn to achieve Spirit Freedom by using other strategies such as Neurological-Linguistic Programming (NLP) techniques of positivity to change your perception of the whole world. You will also learn to understand how mind over matter allows you to make wise choices in your life, trusting in our Heavenly Father and His plan for you. You will be able to access the power of the Holy Ghost to know what to do next in order to live the best life you can!

"Approximately 1.5 of the 7.9 billion people on this planet live under communist government leadership, that's 19% of the world population who may not have the liberty to choose their preference for religious worship, education, or career." (Rosenberg, M. 2019; World Population Review, 2020)

Another influential individual who impacted my life, Joseph B. Wirthlin, an apostle of the Lord, in this dispensation, said this powerful quote:

"Create a masterpiece of your life. No matter our age, circumstances, or abilities, each one of us can create something remarkable of his (her) life." (Wirthlin, J.B., 2006)

One of the most important lessons I learned as a child is that "A victim mentality defeats the liberty to choose!" We all have the power to choose the right way to live, the right path to follow and the right mindset to have. A victim blames everyone for what's happened to them, but it takes courage to move beyond the bad experiences, learn from them and rise above it to create something wonderful of our lives. We can choose to take responsibility for our choices!

The choices we make every day, good or bad can change our future. Great choices bring great outcomes, while bad choices bring undesirable outcomes. If you are living in a country that allows you the liberty to choose how you worship, the career you desire and the life you want to live, remember you are fortunate and among the approximate 81% of the world's population that have more freedom to choose. Regardless of what country you may live in, everyone has the ability to choose spiritual freedom. Understanding this power allows you to feel true Spirit Freedom!

Another favourite verse in the Holy Bible in the Book of Proverbs written by King Solomon tells us to,

5 *Trust in the Lord with all thine heart; and lean not unto thine own understanding.*

Choice

***6** In all thy ways acknowledge him, and he shall direct thy paths. (King James Version, Proverbs 3:5-6)*

Live your best life; create the life that leaves a great legacy for others to look to for love, hope, positivity, peace, joy and guidance! I remember seeing certain individuals with a white aura or glow around them. They were usually kind, loving, and compassionate towards others and particularly to my family growing up. This ability to notice this aura or glow around people inspired me to strive to be like them. I particularly was aware of their expression in words which were positive, uplifting and encouraging. I remember making a conscious choice and effort to do all I could to have this same aura, glow or countenance they possessed, and this meant helping my parents, siblings, and other children around me.

The day I was baptised was unforgettable. It was a day I looked forward to and prepared for since my spiritual experience at seven. It was on Sunday 6th April 1980 and what made it even more special was that I was getting baptised with my sister, Sarai, who had just turned eight in March. I remember walking down the stairs into the baptismal font dressed in white, so excited and knowing with all my heart that this was the absolute right choice to make, to follow my Saviour Jesus Christ's example and make this my lifelong commitment. My dad, having been given the priesthood (power and authority of God), baptised us. After coming out of the water; I felt so much peace and love! After we had changed out of our wet clothes, I remember him placing his hands upon our heads, and bestowing upon us, the Gift of the Holy Ghost. Sharing that experience with my sister, Sarai, was memorable and special!

I will always remember, treasure and hold close to my heart when my parents were struggling financially to provide for our family due to difficult economic times, and I would try my best to help them out. My dad became ill at times, exhausted from working three jobs and sometimes making $20 a week in the late 70s, which was not a lot of money to live on, especially with a large and growing family, a mortgage and other bills to pay, yet he was persistent and determined.

For the next couple of years, I had developed a passion for baking and baked cookies, pies and cakes to sell in our neighbourhood for 50 cents each. I was happy that in some way or another I could contribute to our family's wellbeing and welfare. That was my first taste of entrepreneurship! I also remembered at around ten years old, after doing my homework, and once my siblings had gone to sleep, I would stay up and help my mother weave baskets during the night. I learned how to weave cane baskets and make twine pot plant holders that hung from hooks in the ceiling. I treasured those moments with my mother as we worked during the night. It was difficult, and sometimes my fingers would hurt, but I knew that it was to help my family and I found joy in doing that. My mum and I would make close to $60 a week making 60 baskets or pot plant holders. I understood that good choices and sacrifice brought joy, happiness, accomplishment and satisfaction.

My recent studies and research in Neurological Linguistic Programming presents strategies that I was guided to through the power of the Holy Ghost growing up. Specific studies show the incredible power of our minds, the words we use and how positive visualisations impact our reality and environments each day. I remember telling myself that everyone goes through their own problems which affect their reactions in any given situation. Instead of reacting negatively to people, things, and situations around me, I would try to understand where they were coming from. Mentally, this not only helped me to feel happiness and love within myself, but I was able to automatically feel compassion towards other people around me.

Every positive choice I made in my home helped me to feel peace, joy, happiness and closeness to our Heavenly Father, Jesus Christ and the Holy Ghost. This is what brings true Spirit Freedom!

If you're wondering why the concept "choice" is important, every day we make choices, and there are consequences to those choices. Positive choices bring positive consequences, while negative choices bring negative consequences or outcomes. Which would we prefer?

In the world we live in, there can be tremendous stress, expectations, and sometimes our natural tendencies are to think negative thoughts, use negative words and do negative things. This is precisely why we need to consciously start the day with a positive mindset, a goal for ourselves to think positive thoughts, say positive things and do more good around us. The most important thing to remember is that you can do it! Believe in your power to choose, to create and to live a life of purpose, a happy, fulfilled and exciting life. It may be hard to start, but the important thing to remember is that the conscious effort to begin is so worth it in the end.

Through NLP strategies and the power of the Holy Ghost, I encourage you to apply some of these strategies daily:

1. Choose **3** <u>positive</u> visuals, images, dreams or experiences each morning and make a conscious decision to be happy! (There are a few examples of affirmations, vision board or dream board, and lists of positive words in the back of my book for you).

2. Each morning choose **3** positive words to say out loud about yourself, **3** positive thoughts you will think about yourself, and **3** positive actions you will apply today to help yourself.

3. Choose **3** talents, interests or passions, write them down and how you're going to improve, develop it or begin learning about them today! (**Power of 3**)

We have the liberty to choose to be kind, good, happy and positive. Ask yourself, "What can I do today to improve myself and help others? Choose to be happy in word and deed! If it makes you feel good, happy and love, than do it!

-Taloa Walters

CHAPTER 4

Worthy Music has Power to make us Humble,

Prayerful and Grateful.

-Russell M. Nelson

We can access the power of strength through worthy music. In this chapter, you will understand the power of worthy music and how it unlocks spirituality. Worthy music is songs, musical compositions, or combinations of sounds that possess the power to connect, resonate, lift and inspire your spirit to connect with God and to other people around you. Worthy music truly is a universal language of the soul, of angels, stimulating optical cognitive function and ultimate emotional intelligence! You will also see how worthy music has the ability to protect you and opens your mind to realise miracles each day as you apply it into your life!

In a paper written in 2011 "The Power of Music to Affect the Brain: NPR", it advises that listening to music can make you feel more relaxed, and in some cultures, it's even used to ease pain. Science all but confirms that humans are hard-wired to respond to music. Studies also suggest that someday music may even help patients heal from Parkinson's disease or a stroke (www.npr.org) (NPR, 2011). In my early childhood studies, babies' brains were stimulated and responded to music being played. I loved playing worthy music before my children were born, after giving birth to them, and throughout my children's early childhood years. I've seen the benefits of worthy music in my own life and within the lives of my children and family.

I love this quote by President Russell M. Nelson, the 17th President of The Church of Jesus Christ of Latter Day Saints since the restoration of the church, who is a world-renowned heart surgeon and one of the pioneers of a research team that developed the heart/lung machine making it possible to perform the first open heart bypass surgery in 1951. He said that,

"Worthy music has power to make us humble, prayerful and grateful....You will be spiritually stronger if you do." (Nelson, R. M., 2008)

A wonderful woman, Rosemary M. Wixon, called as the 12th General Primary President in The Church of Jesus Christ of Latter Day Saints, in a speech given in 2013 said that music,

"..Enhances our senses, touches our emotions and creates memories." (Wixon, R. M., 2013).

I felt this connection in my home as a young child growing up. My father loved music and had perfect pitch, playing music by ear on the guitar. He would listen to music people would play and then would play it on the guitar and sing the lyrics. That's how powerful worthy music is! I discovered that worthy music became another channel of spiritual communication with my Heavenly Father. The lessons I learned through worthy music led to developing positivity in hymns played on the church organ since the age of ten.

Power

Choosing to think positive thoughts, using positive words and remembering scriptures that I read with my family was another way I connected to our Heavenly Father and His love for me. The proverb found in the Holy Bible, Book of Proverbs, written by King Solomon said,

"As [a man] thinketh in his heart, so is he." (King James Version, Proverbs 23:7)

President Russell M. Nelson also said,

"As you control your thoughts, you control your actions. Indeed, worthy music can provide power and protection for the soul." (Nelson, R.M., 2008).

Without the power and protection of worthy music, spirituality is locked and cannot truly be accessed. Worthy music unlocks spiritual power and protection within us, allowing miracles to be heard, seen and experienced in life.

Later I read this, and it penetrated my heart,

"If thou art merry, praise the Lord with singing, with music, with dancing, and with a prayer of praise and thanksgiving." (Doctrine and Covenants, Section 136:28)

Also, in another scripture the Lord says,

"For my soul delighteth in the song of the heart; yea, the song of the righteous is a prayer unto me, and it shall be answered with a blessing upon their heads." (Doctrine and Covenants, Section 25:12)

These scriptures helped me understand my spiritual connection with our Heavenly Father in the positive feelings I felt through worthy music! My parents loved to sing hymns and constantly sang while they were doing things around our home; chores, gardening, preparing food, and family prayers. Through worthy music, I found strength and protection.

In creating an environment of worthy music within our home, my parents made the sacrifice to provide piano lessons for my siblings and me. My parents found a piano teacher, Fofoga, who was from the same Samoan island where my dad was raised, Savai'i. I remember my first Samoan hymn, "Ia Fiafia Pea" literal English translation, "Be Happy," held so much spiritual significance in my life at that time. Through music I could express how I felt deep inside that words could not explain.

Although the learning process was challenging for me, the effort required to learn to play the piano helped me understand the process of hard work, persistence, faith, determination and complete surrender to our Heavenly Father, trusting that He would be there to make up for the rest of what I couldn't do alone. Through worthy music, I learned how to unlock the powers of heaven, obtain treasures of knowledge, and uncover the mysteries of God. Worthy music was the key to that! I learned that exercising faith involved complete trust in our Heavenly Father and exerting tremendous effort on my part. The miracles I experienced daily were the power to overcome my weaknesses, the spiritual strength I felt that was beyond imagination and the spiritual protection from mental darkness and negativity.

A courageous young man, Moroni in the Book of Mormon marvels at this incredible power when he expresses,

> *"And now, I Moroni would speak somewhat concerning these things; I would show unto the world that faith is things which are hoped for and not seen; wherefore, dispute not because ye seen not, for ye receive no witness until after the trial of your faith." (Book of Mormon, Ether 12:6)*

Later in that same chapter, he continues to remind us how the Lord teaches us when we allow it,

Power

"And if men come unto me I will show unto them their weakness. I give unto men weakness that they may be humble; and my grace is sufficient for all men that humble themselves before me; for if they humble themselves before me, and have faith in me, then will I make weak things become strong unto them." (Book of Mormon, Ether 12:27)

I remember that 1982 was a busy year; learning to play music led to spiritually prepare to go with my family to the Hamilton New Zealand Temple to be sealed as a family for all eternity. I knew at that time that financially it was a great sacrifice for my parents, but it was definitely worth everything. After all I had learned about the Eternal Plan of Happiness, I looked forward to this blessing. I loved my family so much, and one of my greatest desires was that my relationships with my parents and siblings would continue after death. Through continuous revelation to a living prophet and the restoration of the Lord's church in The Church of Jesus Christ of Latter Day Saints, the power of God to perform these saving ordinances were on the earth again since the great apostasy. The temple is the Lord's house on earth where we make covenants with him through restored priesthood authority and power from our Heavenly Father. That memory is so vivid in my mind to this day. I remember being dressed in white with my whole family; it was so special, sacred and beautiful. Everything around me was so magnificent and peaceful, and I was filled with love. Being in the Temple was like being home, my heavenly home. I was overwhelmed with love, joy and happiness filling my whole body, and I knew that our Heavenly Father and Jesus Christ loved my family and me in such a powerful and indescribable way.

My mum was inspired to send my dad on a holiday for his birthday that same year. Dad needed a break from working so hard. She worked during the nights and saved money, and in August she surprised him with a plane ticket to Australia for his birthday gift. He stayed with relatives in Bankstown, New South Wales.

On his second day in Australia, Dad came across a factory, Dunlop Shoe Company, and enquired about a job. He was hired immediately and started that Friday. There were five casual workers hired, and they all started on the same day. My dad had a charismatic and friendly way with people; he was raised in a harsh environment of plantation life in Samoa and developed a strong endurance to hard work, and had efficient and effective work ethics. Each week at work, one of the casuals he started with was let go, and at the end of the fourth week, he thought for sure he was next to leave. He planned to travel back to New Zealand to us the following Tuesday. I remember missing my dad a lot during the time he was away. At the end of that week, Dad's boss said to him, "You are the kind of worker I'm looking for," and from that day on, my dad was a permanent employee. My dad explained that he needed to return to his family in New Zealand and his boss told him that he could work there until he was ready to leave to get his family and that he would hold the position for him until he got back, which he did.

There was constant communication between my parents, and I could feel the excitement of moving to a new country and a new beginning for all of us. I remember my dad exclaiming several years later that Australia was the 'promised land'. My dad's new job paid more than the three jobs combined in New Zealand, and he was overjoyed for the opportunities that lay ahead for our family. My dad continued to work in Australia for another couple of months, saving for our family's move, and returned in October. In the meantime, my grandmothers lived with us, and my mother decided to get a job to help with moving expenses. It was a huge move! My mum had a mind of her own and against my dad's wishes, had a goal to be a little more financially prepared.

My parents were 'cut from the same cloth' and were resourceful, hardworking and goal-oriented. Shortly after my father had expressed his excitement for the family to move, my mum pursued a job at the new electrical wiring factory in town. She walked in, interviewed for the job and got a call back that she was hired. She had not had a job for ten years. Before that, she worked for five years at the New Zealand Towel Company, since arriving from Samoa at the age of 22, and before that she was a Samoan school teacher, straight out of high school.

Power

Mum started work and saved for our move. We stayed home with our grandmothers, Tina (Mum's mother) and Si'i (Dad's mother) who we loved and cherished. We learned so much from them. Although they were the adults, my siblings and I did everything else as we were quite independent. My mum taught me how to cook when I was eight, so I would help with lunches for my siblings, and we all helped each other do what needed to be done to help our family. When my dad returned, my grandmothers travelled back to Samoa and we started packing our things in preparation for our big move to Australia. I appreciated and was so grateful for my parents' amazing example of hard work, determination and faith in the Lord. I know that it was the source of many of our blessings.

My parents worked together to tie up loose ends and finalise all our plans for moving. My mother continued to work until the day before we got on the plane. It was hectic, and I was so relieved when everything was packed and we were ready to leave. I remember helping my dad and my siblings organise our things while Mum was at work. I recall being so excited to get on the plane on the 23rd of December 1982. I had just turned 11, and I was so happy and in awe of what was about to happen. I remember sitting by the window watching the plane lift off. That was the beginning of my love of travel and adventure! I had 'gotten bitten by the travel bug' which affected several of my choices later in life.

You're probably wondering how this all has to do with the power of music, but I'm getting there! We arrived in Australia, and I remember the heatwave that greeted us when we stepped off the plane. I also remember going to the fruit market and being blown away from the abundance of food, including food I had never seen before. Everything was inexpensive, and it was like experiencing the 'promised land' in the scriptures where obedience to the Lord's commandments brought prosperity to many people and nations. I felt wealthy, rich and that I was living a dream…anything was possible!

That same week we moved to Australia, we settled in the Bankstown area and went to church, and I was called on to play the organ for our ward (church congregation). I'm reminded of the concept, 'where much is given, much is required'. I felt I had been blessed so much in my life so far and volunteering to play for church was the least I could do to give back to our Heavenly Father and the community of people that helped us transition to Australia. Playing piano each Sunday for church was scary because at the time, I could only play one hymn (Ia Fiafia Pea – Be Happy) and to avoid the embarrassment of making mistakes on the huge, loud organ, I would prayerfully practice hymns endlessly every spare moment before school, after school, after homework and after chores in preparation for Sunday. Sometimes I felt like everyone at home was sick of listening to me practice, but in reality, it created an environment of happiness, joy, motivation, perseverance, determination and faith in the Lord. I found that out later from my parents. The hymns I practised encouraged my family to sing along. There was no complaint from anyone, just my own insecurities, doubts and sometimes frustration. I learned to be more patient, have more trust and exercise more faith. My mistakes were less and less each week during church and the hymns I learned and played became my sanctuary, peace, comfort and gentle education through the Holy Ghost from our loving Heavenly Father which brought miracles daily. I believed that the best teacher is our Heavenly Father who knows all things and is the source of all knowledge.

My relationship with our Heavenly Father and Jesus Christ strengthened through the Holy Ghost in learning to play worthy music! It became my spiritual language of communication with them. Soon I was able to play over 300 hymns, and the process became a little easier. It wasn't until several years later in high school that my parents found Don Newton, an incredible piano teacher, musician and an inspiration to me, who introduced and expanded my repertoire of worthy music to classical and other inspiring music of worship. He was devoted to the Lord, had an exceptional music talent, was extremely patient, and had unconditional faith in me. I'm grateful to other friends who also were and are wonderful inspiration in music expression, such as Luke, Faiva, Lilieta, and Joe, to name a few. Many other miracles came into my life through worthy music.

Power

If you're wondering what is worthy music, it's either vocal, instrumental or both united to create sounds of beauty, harmony and emotional expression. Music is an art form with elements of pitch, rhythm, dynamic, timbre and texture. Worthy music uplifts, enlightens, and promotes positive feelings, thoughts, and actions.

You may be wondering why worthy music instead of any other genre of music? For me, worthy music was specifically hymns as it was predominantly what I listened to, sang and played throughout my childhood/teenage years. It was the vehicle allowing daily connection to the power of love, communication and connection to our Heavenly Father. The words of the hymns I devoted my childhood learning to play penetrated my heart, teaching me about the nature of our Heavenly Father, the power of healing through the Atonement of Christ and their unconditional love for me, helping me to grow, learn, and develop in character from the inside out.

Worthy music reinforced the unconditional love of our Heavenly Father and Jesus Christ for us. As I embraced other worthy music, such as classical, jazz, relaxation and contemporary songs written on topics of heartfelt love, hope, inspiration and optimism, my awareness of miracles heightened and expanded during those valuable childhood and teenage years!

I hope that you will take up a challenge to implement the following:
1. Choose to listen to worthy music daily (suggestions in the back of my book)
2. Sing, learn a musical instrument or study worthy music
3. Reflect and journal how you feel as you listen, sing or play worthy music daily.

Worthy music communicates our deepest love, devotion and gratitude to our Heavenly Father, our Saviour, Jesus Christ and other people through the power of the Holy Ghost.

-Taloa Walters

CHAPTER 5

Pure Intelligence can be spoken into the mind,

the Holy Ghost communicates with our spirits through the

mind more than through the physical senses.

-Boyd K. Packer

We can strengthen our relationships of trust with Heavenly Father, Jesus Christ, others, our surroundings and within ourselves. Within this chapter, you will come to understand your true divine heritage, a child of God. You will come to understand that our Heavenly Father is the source of all knowledge; you will discover your spiritual ability to completely and wholeheartedly trust in Him. Through humility, you will access that power within you to connect with our Heavenly Father and feel his unconditional love for you. Complete submission to your Heavenly Father's will brings you spiritually closer to Him and accepting that you are worth everything to Him! Through Christ's atoning sacrifice, you will recognise that you are part of his divine and eternal family, and discover the strength, courage and power within you to succeed in all your righteous pursuits. This spiritual connection to our Heavenly Father, to everyone around you, and everything that surrounds you will be realised through the transcendent communicative power of the Holy Ghost or the Holy Spirit of God. Heavenly Father, Jesus Christ and the Holy Ghost are the Godhead.

An interesting fact is that Christianity is the leading global religion in 2020. Christians make up approximately 29% of the world population, and this is increasing. In a prophecy in the bible, all will come to know Christ and Heavenly Father who sent Him, and in the words of one called of God as the 15th prophet in The Church of Jesus Christ of Latter Day Saints at the October general conference of 2007, President Gordon B. Hinckley said,

> *"The Church has become one large family scattered across the earth. There are now more than 13 million of us in 176 nations and territories. A marvellous and wonderful thing is coming to pass. The Lord is fulfilling His promise that His gospel shall be as the stone cut out of the mountain without hands which would roll forth and fill the whole earth, as Daniel saw in vision (see Daniel 2:31-45; Doctrine and Covenants Section 65:2) A great miracle is taking place right before our eyes." (Hinckley, G. B., 2007).*

It is through the power of the Holy Ghost or Holy Spirit that this can happen. The Holy Ghost communicates to our spirits of truth, Heavenly Father's purposes and our individual missions on this earth. Another wonderful prophet of this dispensation and the 13th President of the Church of Jesus Christ of Latter Day Saints, President Ezra Taft Benson said this about the Holy Ghost,

> *"The Holy Ghost causes our feelings to be more tender (tenderer). We feel more charitable and compassionate with each other. We are more calm (calmer) in our relationships. We have a greater*

capacity to love each other. People want to be around us because our very countenances radiate the influence of the Spirit. We are more godly (godlier) in our character. As a result, we become increasingly more sensitive to the promptings of the Holy Ghost and thus able to comprehend spiritual things more clearly." (Idlehearts, 2020).

Without the connection to the Holy Ghost or spirit of God, communication and guidance are challenging. Learning to understand ourselves is essential and crucial to progression. To truly learn about ourselves and the path to take, connection and communication with our Heavenly Father are essential through the power of the Holy Ghost. By understanding the Godhead, we can be led to understanding our purpose and mission in life. It also provides for true submission to our Heavenly Father's will, understanding that we belong to his eternal family and that as our Heavenly Father loves us dearly and wants us to return to Him some day. He promises to refine us through trials, afflictions and weaknesses so that we become the best version of ourselves and achieve our ultimate potential on earth and into the eternities.

In the Holy Bible from the words of John, one of the apostles chosen by Jesus Christ to help Peter and James lead the church after his death wrote what Jesus Christ taught them about the Holy Ghost,

"But the Comforter, which is the Holy Ghost, whom the Father will send in my name, he shall teach you all things, and bring all things to your remembrance, whatsoever I have said unto you." (King James Version, John 14:26)

It is only through the power of the Holy Ghost that we can understand the scriptures, the will of our Heavenly Father, how Jesus Christ's atonement changes our hearts and how we can understand our uniqueness, talents, gifts and purposes in life. Although our Heavenly Father and Jesus Christ have bodies of flesh and bones, the Holy Ghost doesn't because of His divine mission. The Godhead is one in purpose, and the Holy Ghost has several roles to help us keep the commandments and receive the blessings from our Heavenly Father. The Godhead works together to help each of us return to our Heavenly Home.

A great man named Nephi in the Book of Mormon said that the Holy Ghost witnesses to us of our Heavenly Father and Jesus Christ,

> *18 And then are ye in this strait and narrow path which leads to eternal life; yea, ye have entered in by the gate; ye have done according to the commandments of the Father and the Son; and ye have received the Holy Ghost, which witnesses of the Father and the Son, unto the fulfilling of the promise which he hath made, that if ye entered in by the way ye should receive. (Book of Mormon, 2 Nephi 31:18)*

Then another great young man, Moroni said that the Holy Ghost will reveal and teach the truth of all things to us. I had always felt that the Book of Mormon was true, but I had realised that I needed to find out for myself if it was true and to ask my Heavenly Father if it was true. After reading the Book of Mormon from cover to cover, I specifically took Moroni's invitation to ask Heavenly Father if The Book of Mormon was true.

> *3 Behold, I would exhort you that when ye shall read these things, if it be wisdom in God that ye should read them, that ye would remember how merciful the Lord hath been unto the children of men, from the creation of Adam even down until the time that ye shall receive these things, and ponder it in your hearts.*
> *4 And when ye shall receive these things, I would exhort you that ye would ask God, the Eternal Father, in the name of Christ, if these things are not true; and if ye shall ask with a sincere heart with real intent, having faith in Christ, he will manifest the truth of it unto you, by the power of the Holy Ghost.*
> *5 And by the power of the Holy Ghost ye may know the truth of all things.*
> *6 And whatsoever thing is good is just and true; wherefore, nothing that is good denieth the Christ, but acknowledgeth that he is. (Book of Mormon, Moroni 10:3-6)*

The answer I received was not only the feeling of love from my Heavenly Father but the personal feeling that Moroni was real and that the words he wrote in the Book of Mormon were written for me. The impression was so strong that my heart was overflowing with love for this great man, who lived approximately 1600 years ago, who saw a vision of us, and kept the Lord's commandments to preserve this ancient record so that we could read it and know that Heavenly Father, Jesus Christ and the Holy Ghost live and love us. I couldn't hold back the tears. Even as I recall and share this experience with you, my eyes are welling up with tears. Those impressions and feelings were from the Holy Ghost touching my heart and letting me know that The Book of Mormon was the word of God, another testament to the world along with the Bible that Heavenly Father, Jesus Christ and the Holy Ghost exist, are real and want the best for each of us.

Once I knew the Book of Mormon was the word of God, it strengthened my faith that Joseph Smith who translated it was a prophet called by God and that The Church of Jesus Christ of Latter Days was the Lord's restored church and kingdom on earth. Recently, a proclamation to the world was shared by our living prophet today, President Russell M. Nelson and the apostles which states,

THE RESTORATION OF THE FULNESS OF THE GOSPEL OF JESUS CHRIST: A BICENTENNIAL PROCLAMATION TO THE WORLD

The First Presidency and Council of the Twelve Apostles of The Church of Jesus Christ of Latter-day Saints

We solemnly proclaim that God loves His children in every nation of the world. God the Father has given us the divine birth, the incomparable life, and the infinite atoning sacrifice of His Beloved Son, Jesus Christ. By the power of the Father, Jesus rose again and gained the victory over death. He is our Saviour, our Exemplar, and our Redeemer. Two hundred years ago, on a beautiful spring morning in 1820, young Joseph Smith, seeking to know which church to join, went into the woods to pray near his home in upstate New York, USA. He had questions regarding the salvation of his soul and trusted that God would direct him. In humility, we declare that in answer to his prayer, God the Father and His Son, Jesus Christ, appeared to Joseph and inaugurated the "restitution of all things" (Acts 3:21) as foretold in the Bible. In this vision, he learned that following the death of the original Apostles, Christ's New Testament Church was lost from the earth. Joseph would be instrumental in its return. We affirm that under the direction of the Father and the Son, heavenly messengers came to instruct Joseph and re-establish the Church of Jesus Christ. The resurrected John the Baptist restored the authority to baptize by immersion for the remission of sins. Three of the original twelve Apostles—Peter, James, and John—restored the apostleship and keys of priesthood authority. Others came as well, including Elijah, who restored the authority to join families together forever in eternal relationships that transcend death. We further witness that Joseph Smith was given the gift and power of God to translate an ancient record: the Book of Mormon—Another Testament of Jesus Christ. Pages of this sacred text include an account of the personal ministry of Jesus Christ among people in the Western Hemisphere soon after His Resurrection. It teaches of life's purpose and explains the doctrine of Christ, which is central to that purpose. As a companion scripture to the Bible, the Book of Mormon testifies that all human beings are sons and daughters of a loving Father in Heaven, that He has a divine plan for our lives, and that His Son, Jesus Christ, speaks today as well as in days of old. We declare that The Church of Jesus Christ of Latter Day Saints, organized on April 6, 1830, and is Christ's New Testament Church restored. This Church is anchored in the perfect life of its chief cornerstone, Jesus Christ, and in His infinite Atonement and literal Resurrection. Jesus Christ has once again called Apostles and has given them priesthood authority. He invites all of us to come unto Him and His Church, to receive the Holy

Ghost, the ordinances of salvation, and to gain enduring joy. Two hundred years have now elapsed since this Restoration was initiated by God the Father and His Beloved Son, Jesus Christ. Millions throughout the world have embraced knowledge of these prophesied events. We gladly declare that the promised Restoration goes forward through continuing revelation. The earth will never again be the same, as God will "gather together in one all things in Christ" (Ephesians 1:10). With reverence and gratitude, we as His Apostles invite all to know—as we do—that the heavens are open. We affirm that God is making known His will for His beloved sons and daughters. We testify that those who prayerfully study the message of the Restoration and act in faith will be blessed to gain their own witness of its divinity and of its purpose to prepare the world for the promised Second Coming of our Lord and Saviour, Jesus Christ.
(LDS, 2020)

As I continued my volunteer service in The Church of Jesus Christ of Latter Day Saints, first as an organist since the age of 11 for the different wards (congregations) I moved to, then as a youth leader in the Young Women's Program, and a Relief Society teacher in the Parramatta ward after I graduated from high school, I continued to feel the love of my Heavenly Father and redeeming peace of Jesus Christ just as I first experienced it when I was seven. The love from our Heavenly Father and Jesus Christ was a continuous indication that I was on the right path in following the Eternal Plan of Happiness. Receiving the gift of the Holy Ghost through our Heavenly Father's priesthood power after my baptism at eight allowed me access to continuous communication and personal revelation to guide me throughout my childhood and teenage years.

I'm reminded of one of the scriptures I read with my grandmother at the dining table and later in the Primary program (children ages 18mths -10yrs old), Young Women program (girls ages 11-18), and the Seminary program (4 years of morning scripture class ages 14-18) where Jesus said to his apostle, Thomas;

"Jesus saith unto him, I am the way the truth, and the life: no man cometh unto the Father, but by me." (King James Version, John 14:6)

Jesus Christ set the example for us to follow. Study of his words helps us to know Him and our Heavenly Father and feel their love for us. As Jesus Christ continued to teach his disciples, he describes the perfect law of love to them;

***8** Herein is my Father glorified, that ye bear much fruit; so shall ye be my disciples.*
***9** As the Father hath loved me, so have I loved you: continue ye in my love.*
***10** If ye keep my commandments, ye shall abide in my love; even as I have kept my Father's commandments, and abide in his love.*
***11** These things have I spoken unto you, that my joy might remain in you, and that your joy might be full.*
***12** This is my commandment, that ye love one another, as I have loved you.*
***13** Greater love hath no man than this, that a man lay down his life for his friends.*
***14** Ye are my friends, if ye do whatsoever I command you.*
***15** Henceforth I call you not servants; for the servant knoweth not what his lord doeth: but I have called you friends; for all things that I have heard of my Father I have made known unto you. (King James Version, John 15: 8-15)*

The prophet Nephi shares his last words in the Book of Mormon, encouraging us to follow Jesus Christ's example of baptism by water and baptism by fire, being cleansed by the Holy Ghost. By having the gift of the Holy Ghost, we can access many other gifts for our benefit,

***13** Wherefore, my beloved brethren, I know that if ye shall follow the Son, with full purpose of heart, acting no hypocrisy and no deception before God, but with real intent, repenting of your sins, witnessing unto the Father that ye are willing to take upon you the name of*

Christ, by baptism yea, by following your Lord and your Savior down into the water, according to his word, behold, then shall ye receive the Holy Ghost; yea, then cometh the baptism of fire and of the Holy Ghost; and then can ye speak with the tongue of angels, and shout praises unto the Holy One of Israel. (Book of Mormon, 2 Nephi 31:13)

I love this particular verse that Paul describes many other gifts we can receive through the Holy Ghost as he writes to the church members in Galatians,

__22__ But the fruits of the Spirit is love, peace, longsuffering, gentleness, goodness, faith,
__23__ Meekness, temperance: against such there is no law. (King James Version, Galatians 5:22-23)

Paul's words written to the Corinthians also described how everyone is blessed with different gifts through the power of the Holy Ghost. He said,

__4__ Now there are diversities of gifts, but the same Spirit.
__5__ And there are differences of administrations, but the same Lord.
__6__ And there are diversities of operations, but it is the same God which worketh all in all.
__7__ But the manifestation of the Spirit given to every man to profit withal.
__8__ For to one is given by the Spirit the word of wisdom; to another the word of knowledge by the same Spirit.
__9__ To another faith by the same Spirit; to another the gifts of healing by the same Spirit.
__10__ To another the working of miracles; to another prophecy to another discern of spirits; to another divers kinds of tongues; to another the interpretation of tongue.
__11__ But all these worketh that one and the selfsame Spirit, dividing to every man severally as he will. (King James Version, 1 Corinthians 12:4-11)

Why would you not want the gift of the Holy Ghost? The process of connecting to Heavenly Father, Jesus Christ, to each other and understanding who we truly are is essential to life's true success. We are all born with the natural and innate desire of belonging and to be connected to someone or something. Through the gift of the Holy Ghost, we can fulfil that very desire. We can know that we belong to an incredible, immense, extensive spiritual family with a loving Heavenly Father who loves us all dearly. We can know that through the gift of the Holy Ghost.

I desired to receive this special gift with all my heart, and after receiving it through priesthood authority from my father after my baptism, I began a lifelong process of understanding this gift and how He works in my life each day. We have the ability to succeed in every area of life through the gift of the Holy Ghost by merely asking our Heavenly Father for help. He answers us through the power of the Holy Ghost. The more effort we place on these desires, goals in life, purposes and dreams having faith in Christ, we will achieve ultimate success in life through the gift of the Holy Ghost.

Why is it important to understand who the Holy Ghost is and what His purpose is? I've come to understand that through the Spirit of God, Holy Spirit or Holy Ghost, we can physically feel and experience the power of Heavenly Father's love, forgiveness, peace, and happiness. Understanding that the Holy Ghost is how our Heavenly Father and Jesus Christ communicate with us without being physically present is the very purpose and reason why He is a personage of Spirit. Although Heavenly Father, Jesus Christ and the Holy Ghost are separate beings, they have the same purpose; to help all of our Heavenly Father's children return to our Heavenly Home.

Christ's words in his prayer indicate the importance of prayer, his purpose on earth and learning about him in these following verses,

> *1 These words spake Jesus, and lifted up his eyes to heaven, and said, Father, the hour is come; glorify thy Son, that thy Son also may glorify thee:*
> *2 As thou hast given him power over all flesh, that he should give eternal life to as many as thou hast given him.*

Connect

3 And this is life eternal, that they might know thee the only true God, and Jesus Christ, whom thou hast sent.
4 I have glorified thee on the earth: I have finished the work which thou gavest me to do.
5 And now, O Father, glorify thou me with thine own self with the glory which I had with thee before world was. (King James Version, John 17:1-5)

In addition to this, in the Pearl of Great Price, the Book of Moses, the Lord speaks directly to him and explains,

39 For behold, this is my work and my glory to bring to pass the immortality and eternal life of man. (Pearl of Great Price, Moses 1:39)

One of the things I'm so grateful for is that our Heavenly Father provides many sources for us to learn more about Him, His love for us, His purposes and how to discover our purpose in life not only from the Holy Bible which is a record of the descendants of Judah, one of the tribes of Israel but also from the Book of Mormon, another record of the descendants of Joseph, another tribe of Israel and their dealings with our Heavenly Father. We now have the privilege of possessing other records; The Pearl of Great Price, containing revelation given to the prophet Joseph Smith from our Heavenly Father with regards to His commandments, comprising the Book of Moses; the Book of Abraham, from some Egyptian papyri that Joseph Smith was commanded to translate containing the communication between Heavenly Father, Jesus Christ and the patriarch, Abraham.

Having these sources at our fingertips makes it possible for us to fully understand the Gospel of Jesus Christ in The Church of Jesus Christ of Latter Day Saints.

Our Heavenly Father and Jesus Christ's ability to communicate with us through the power of the Holy Ghost with more people at the same time is immeasurable and incomprehensible, yet absolutely possible. It is the very essence of His being and purpose, to communicate spirit to spirit. The Holy Ghost has the power to communicate with our spirits. Further explanation of how the Holy Ghost works is found in John when Christ explains,

> **13** *Howbeit when he, the Spirit is come, he will guide you into all truth: for he shall not speak of himself; but whatsoever he shall hear, that shall he speak: and he will shew you things to come. (King James Version, John 16:13)*

Through the Holy Ghost, we will understand that each of us is part of our Heavenly Father's family and the Godhead is one in purpose. Through Jesus Christ, we can be sanctified. This is evident in Christ's words that the Holy Ghost reveals truth and is truth,

> **17** *Sanctify them through thy truth: thy word is truth.*
> **18** *As thou hast sent me into the world, even so have I also sent them into the world.*
> **19** *And for their sakes I sanctify myself, that they also might be sanctified through the truth.*
> **20** *Neither pray I for these alone, but for them also which shall believe on me through their word.*
> **21** *That they all may be one as thou, Father, art in me, and I in thee, that they also may be one in us: that the world may believe that thou hast sent me.*
> **22** *And the glory which thou gavest me I have given them; that they may be one, even as we are one.*
> **23** *I in them, and thou in me, that they may be made perfect in one; and that the world may know that thou hast sent me, and hast loved them, as thou hast loved me.*
> **24** *Father, I will that they also, whom thou hast given me, be with me where I am; that they may behold my glory, which thou hast given me: for thou lovedst me before the foundation of the world.*
> **25** *O righteous Father, the world hath not known thee: but I have known thee, and these have known that thou hast sent me.*

26 *And I have declared unto them thy name, and will declare it: that the love wherewith thou hast loved me may be in them, and I in them.*
(King James Version, John 17:17-26)

There is additional explanation in the Book of Mormon by the prophet Jacob,

13 *Behold, my brethren, he that prophesieth, let him prophesy to the understanding of men; for the Spirit speaketh the truth and lieth not. Wherefore, it speaketh of things as they really are, and of the things as they really will be; wherefore, these things are manifested unto us plainly, for the salvation of our souls. But behold, we are not witnesses alone in these things; for God also spake them unto prophets of old. (Book of Mormon, Jacob 4:13)*

Everyone who was born since Adam and Eve, and those who are living on the earth now, as well as those who are yet to be born in the future, exist as spirit children of our Heavenly Father. As discussed in the Eternal Plan of Happiness in Chapter 2, we existed before this world, and our purpose on earth is to learn progress and prepare to return to our heavenly home. We can feel the love of our Heavenly Father and Jesus Christ through the power of the Holy Ghost and understand that our relationships with our Heavenly Father and Jesus Christ can continue to grow as we study his word and follow Christ's example.

The apostle Paul wrote to the Galatians expressing this same sentiment,

20 *I am crucified with Christ: nevertheless I live; yet not I, but Christ liveth in me: and the life which I now live in the flesh I live by the faith of the Son of God, who loved me, and gave himself for me. (King James Version, Galatians 2:20)*

Another young man named Alma converted to the gospel of Jesus Christ exclaims in the Book of Mormon,

14 *And now behold, I ask of you, my brethren of the church, have ye spiritually been born of God? Have ye received his image in your countenances? Have ye experienced this mighty change in your hearts? (Book of Mormon, Alma 5: 14)*

The influence of the Holy Ghost can be felt by everyone; he will help us gain a desire to learn about our Heavenly Father and Jesus Christ, yet it is up to us to choose to learn more about his Eternal Plan of Happiness, to be baptised into his church, receive the gift of the Holy Ghost, access true success in life and be guided back to our Heavenly Home.

Connecting with others on our journey back home expands our experience and learning because of the different gifts and talents we can all possess through the power of the Holy Ghost. I will expand more on this in the next few chapters. I'm going to extend a challenge to you right now. Ask yourself this question, how do you feel about all you've learned so far?

If you feel good, happy, enlightened or positive about this information, then continue to follow the next few steps.

1. Listen to the influence of the Holy Ghost daily and focus on that (feelings of joy, happiness, peace, comfort, good, positive) no matter what happens throughout the day.
2. Allow the influence of the Holy Ghost to guide you to do positive things, say positive things, watch and listen to positive things throughout the day.
3. Pray each morning to ask Heavenly Father's help for you to be aware of the influence of the Holy Ghost throughout the day, pay attention to the miracles that happen and thank Heavenly Father for the miracles each night.

Connect

The Holy Ghost is the comforter, teacher, communicator, power and companion of my spirit.

Taloa Walters

CHAPTER 6

Grateful

Gratitude is said to be the memory of the Heart.

-Joseph F. Smith

We can develop and strengthen appreciation, respect and gratitude for life and the atoning sacrifice of our Saviour providing the path for us on our individual journeys to return to our Heavenly home where we are promised eternal abundance.

What is gratitude? It is important to understand the definition of gratitude. In the dictionary, gratitude is "quality of being thankful; the readiness to show appreciation and to return kindness or kindnesses." Having gratitude for all we are, all we have and for everything around us are paramount for eternal life (Living with our Heavenly Father, Jesus Christ and our loved one in peace, joy, love and happiness forever).

The attribute and quality of gratitude is the secret to Eternal Abundance, and within this chapter you will come to understand the importance and benefits of this remarkable quality that sustains love, hope and motivation. You will discover the steps in developing gratitude, which is the key to unlock everything. In an article in Psychology Today by Amy Morin, author of 13 Things The Mentally Strong Don't Do, she discusses seven scientifically proven facts about gratitude,

1. *Gratitude opens the door to more relationships in life*
2. *Gratitude improves physical health*
3. *Gratitude improves psychological health*
4. *Gratitude enhances empathy*
5. *Grateful people sleep better*
6. *Gratitude improves self-esteem*
7. *Gratitude improves mental strength (Morin, A. 2015).*

A phenomenal man and prophet of this dispensation, Joseph Fielding Smith, in 1939, said,

"The spirit of gratitude is always pleasant and satisfying because it carries with it a sense of helpfulness to others; it begets love and friendship, and engenders divine influence. Gratitude is said to be the memory of the heart." (Snow, S., 2001)

Bonnie D Parkin, the 14th General Relief Society President in The Church of Jesus Christ of Latter Day Saints shared in her speech, Gratitude, a Path to Happiness when she said,

"Gratitude is a Spirit-filled principle. It opens our minds to a universe permeated with the richness of a living God." (Parkin, B. D., 2007)

Without gratitude, we become lonely, filled with sadness, dissatisfaction, ill, despair and misery. Gratitude is the secret to abundance in all areas of life. The importance and benefits of gratitude bring joy into daily life, mental strength, and happiness in relationships. Remembering to be grateful for all we are blessed with, all we have achieved in our lives and for the hope of limitless opportunities in the future is the key that unlocks the doors to abundance and success.

Grateful

A humble prophet, Alma in the Book of Mormon expresses,

> **38** *That ye contend no more against the Holy Ghost, but that ye receive it, and take upon you the name of Christ; that ye humble yourselves even to the dust, and worship God, in whatsoever place ye may be in, in spirit and in truth; and that ye live in thanksgiving daily, for the many mercies and blessings which he doth bestow upon you. (Book of Mormon, Alma 34:38)*

Feeling gratitude each day for my positive spiritual experience at the age of seven and reliving those powerful emotions of love motivated continuous positive actions, words and deeds growing up. Expressing this gratitude daily to our Heavenly Father in prayer, to my parents for all they have done for me and to everyone that I've had the privilege of meeting, strengthened my relationships and enriched my life daily.

In my teenage years, I had incredible gratitude for the blessings of the Gospel in my life and had a burning desire to share this with all my friends. In an English assignment in school, we were given the liberty to choose a topic that we were passionate about and had the opportunity to give a verbal presentation in front of the class. I prayed for direction and felt strongly about sharing the Eternal Plan of and Happiness with my classmates. The power of the Holy Ghost guided me in what to say, and I shared my passion for the gospel and left a Book of Mormon for each of my classmates, inviting them to read, pray and let me know if they wanted to learn more. I had always been a quiet person, and I don't know if anything came of it, but I'd never felt bolder, more confident, humbler, or more filled with love and gratitude for each individual in that class!

It was gratitude for our Heavenly Father and Jesus Christ's love through the Holy Ghost that helped me in the transitional period of moving to Australia, adjusting to the Australian culture and way of life, learning to play the piano and serve as the ward organist at 11, overcoming bullying and being discriminated against because of my Samoan culture and the colour of my skin, letting go of negative experiences, developing confidence and mental strength to express my faith, and empowered to see the miracles that happened daily in my life.

Why is it important to have and express gratitude? Throughout my life and the personal experiences I have had, I have learned that by developing and expressing gratitude, I received more blessings physically, spiritually, mentally, emotionally and intellectually. It has happened in every aspect of my life, with healing, positivity, physical health, mental strength, education, occupations, family life, business relationships and love.

How can one develop and express gratitude? How is gratitude the secret to abundance? Throughout history, lives have been changed and transformed merely because of gratitude. Expressing gratitude to our Heavenly Father for all the blessings he gives to us and to others for the kindness they extend to us.

King David in the Holy Bible, expressed this gratitude in Psalms,

> **30** *I will praise the name of God with a song, and will magnify him with thanksgiving. (King James Version, Psalms 69:30)*

Also, in the Doctrine and Covenants, a revelation given to Joseph Smith from the Lord in March 1832 explains,

> **19** *And he who receiveth all things with thankfulness shall be made glorious; and the things of this earth shall be added unto him, even as hundred fold, yea, more. (Doctrine and Covenants, Section 78:19)*

Another revelation from the Lord to Joseph Smith, the prophet on March 8, 1831 in the Doctrine and Covenants expresses that eternal abundance is dependent on gratitude and thanksgiving,

> **7** *But ye are commanded in all things to ask of God, who giveth liberally; and that which the Spirit testifies unto you even so I would that ye should do in all holiness of heart, walking uprightly before me, considering the end of your salvation, doing all things*

with prayer and thanksgiving, that ye may not be seduced by evil spirits, or doctrines of devils, or the commandments of men; for some are of men, and others of devils. (Doctrine and Covenants, Section 46:7)

Gratitude and thanksgiving are vital in strengthening relationships with our Heavenly Father, Jesus Christ, Holy Ghost and everyone in our lives. Every time we express gratitude and thanksgiving, we mentally strengthen ourselves and connect to others on a spiritual level as our Heavenly Father's spirit children. Another way to express gratitude to our Heavenly Father and Jesus Christ is by keeping all the commandments. For anyone that has never read the Holy Bible, Book of Mormon, Doctrine and Covenants or the Pearl of Great Price, here are the commandments in short form given to the prophet Moses by the Lord on Mount Sinai,

1. *Thou shalt have no other gods before me*
2. *Thou shalt not make unto thee any graven image*
3. *Thou shalt not take the name of the Lord thy God in vain*
4. *Remember the Sabbath day, to keep it holy.*
5. *Honour thy father and thy mother.*
6. *Thou shalt not kill*
7. *Thou shalt not steal*
8. *Thou shalt not commit adultery*
9. *Thou shalt not bear false witness*
10. *Thou shalt not covet*

To offer additional insight, Lynn A. Mickelsen, of the First Quorum of the Seventy gave a speech to encourage parents to teach children the Ten Commandments in the higher law given by Jesus Christ during his earthly ministry, also including my thoughts,

"Thou shalt have no other gods before me." Heavenly Father lives and He is the literal Father of our spirits. We are created in His image and possess all His attributes in utero. He loves us and wants us to be like Him. He wants us to return to Him one day. We all need to communicate with him through prayer and teach our children to do the same!

"Thou shalt not make unto thee any graven image." Heavenly Father is first, and we need to teach our children to respect and honour Him. Through our examples, we can show our children how to worship Him through selfless service to others, in family prayer, family home evening and church worship. We do not honour Him by making sports, academics, entertainment, wealth, vanity, or anything else of this world priority over Him.

1. "Thou shalt have no other gods before me." Heavenly Father lives and He is the literal Father of our spirits. We are created in His image and possess all His attributes in utero. He loves us and wants us to be like Him. He wants us to return to Him one day. We all need to communicate with him through prayer and teach our children to do the same!

2. "Thou shalt not make unto thee any graven image." Heavenly Father is first, and we need to teach our children to respect and honour Him. Through our examples, we can show our children how to worship Him through selfless service to others, in family prayer, family home evening and church worship. We do not honour Him by making sports, academics, entertainment, wealth, vanity, or anything else of this world priority over Him.

3. "Thou shalt not take the name of the Lord thy God in vain." Teach our children to honour His name and use it appropriately. Prepare them to make baptismal covenants and to encourage them to keep these covenants. When we do not keep our covenants to Him and not repent, then we take His name in vain.

4. "Thou shalt honour the Sabbath day to keep it holy." We should set aside the Sabbath day to learn of Him, to take our

minds from the worldly chores and worries, to remember him and dedicate time to Him by focusing our hearts and minds on the purpose of our existence. A day that we can become more like Him.

5. "Honour thy father and thy mother." We can choose to show love and respect for our parents regardless of what they have done. We can teach our children to be obedient; train them in the way they should go and they will not depart from it! Our children learn to obey their Heavenly Father by honouring, respecting, and obeying their earthly parents. Encourage family morals and limits of conduct. The Lord will honour his promise of eternal life with our families when we keep this commandment.

6. "Thou shalt not kill." We are created in our Heavenly Father's image. The union of the body with the spirit can bring us a fullness of joy. We need to teach our children to respect the holiness of human life, to respect it and value it. Human life is priceless and a precious stage to eternal life! We must desirously protect it from the moment of conception.

7. "Thou shalt not commit adultery." Our bodies are temples in which our spirits reside and the Spirit of God can dwell! We need to teach our children that our bodies are sacred and should be treated with respect in relation to the family, the splendour of marriage, and the divine nature of procreation our Heavenly Father has gifted us. We enter into a partnership with Him in the creation of life, a power to be respected, protected, and exercised only within the holy bonds of marriage. It is a celestial power that, if abused, will be taken away.

8. "Thou shalt not steal." We should be honest and respect that which belongs to others, especially that which belongs to our

Heavenly Father. We should teach our children by example to pay a full tithing and give generous offerings. When they live with honesty, giving and sharing, they will be filled with joy and the Spirit and power of God.

9. "Thou shalt not bear false witness." We should teach our children by example to tell the truth, to tell things as they really are, to find the good in others, to be positive and kind. Truth is more precious than any earthly possession and the essence of our existence. As we tell the truth, our confidence will wax strong in the presence of God and our fellowman.

10. "Thou shalt not covet." We should teach our children that they are children of God, who loves them. We must love them, and as they feel our love, they will feel Heavenly Father's love too. When they are loved, they feel no need for the possessions of others. Encourage them to rejoice in their personal progress and achievements so they do not compare themselves to others.

Jesus Christ was born and fulfilled the law given to Moses in the Ten Commandments, when a lawyer asked him "which is the greatest commandment in the law?" He responded by saying in Matthew 22:37-40,

> *37 Jesus said unto him, Thou shalt love the Lord thy God with all thy heart, and with all thy soul, and with all thy mind.*
> *38 This is the first and great commandment.*
> *39 And the second is like unto it, Thou shalt love thy neighbor as thyself.*
> *40 On these two commandments hang all the law and the prophets.*
> *(King James Version, Matthew 22:37-40).*

For me, expressing gratitude to our Heavenly Father for his unconditional love for me was to keep all His commandments.

Grateful

Studying his word in the scriptures helped me to know what commandments I needed to keep. Listening to those that loved me and observing the blessings that they received because of their efforts to keep all of our Heavenly Father's commandments set a great example for me to follow as well. Although no one is perfect except for Jesus Christ, our best efforts to keep the commandments is recognised by our Heavenly Father. He promises to bless us according to our efforts. The following steps will help you develop gratitude as they have for me and lead you to the knowledge of eternal abundance, happiness and success in life!

Through an attitude of gratitude and the power of the Holy Ghost, your relationships with our Heavenly Father, Jesus Christ, and others will be enriched, creating a life of success and eternal abundance.

Here are a few suggestions or challenges to develop and express gratitude:

1. As soon as you wake up in the morning express aloud **6** things you're grateful for, e.g., I'm grateful for sleep, my bed, for air, to breathe, life and this beautiful day!
2. Have a journal by your bed and write **6** things you're grateful for, e.g. family, work, beliefs, value, car and home.
3. After expressing gratitude to your Heavenly Father in prayer, express gratitude to **6** people throughout the day, e.g. thank your mum, dad, boss, friend, sister, brother for being there for you!

Gratitude fills my soul as I remember God's miracles in my life, and each time I feel it and express it, more miracles follow.

Taloa Walters

Taloa Walters

Grateful

Parents and Siblings

Center photo: Siaunofo & Tuputala Solitua (Parents)
From Top Left to Right & Around:
Kome, Poasu, Alofa, ME, Sarai, Sii, Petaia, Tina, Tala, Steve, Emosi & Pouniu (Order of oldest to youngest sibling)

CHAPTER 7

Sometimes we just need to see

a greater vision of

what is possible.

-Bonnie L. Oscarson

We can create a vision of who we want to become in all areas of knowledge, development and growth spiritually, physically, mentally, socially, emotionally and intellectually! Have you felt a change of heart from what you've learned so far? I hope that you have applied some of the concepts and strategies I've shared in the last six chapters. Have you noticed any miracles take place in your life lately? I hope you have recognised these miracles and remembered to record these experiences down in your journal.

In this chapter, you will learn how the knowledge of gospel truths, when applied each day, will spiritually prepare you for the uncertainty of the future. You'll discover how by trusting in our Heavenly Father to guide you, you'll receive clarity of vision and personal revelation, spiritually preparing you for what is yet to come. Our Heavenly Father knows each of us extremely well and will provide the pathways and influential people for your vision to be realised. It is important for you to know what you want in order for you to ask for it!

I set five specific goals for the future due to the inspirational examples of the Young Women teachers (organisation in The Church of Jesus Christ of Latter Day Saints for young women from the ages 11 to 17) who were accomplished in their own professions. I was blessed to have church teachers who were doctors, university professors; educated and devoted woman of God who were my personal mentors. I loved them and will always be grateful for their love, for sharing their life stories with me and inspiring me to follow Christ.

Sister Andersen was one of these women from the United States who was serving a temple mission here in Australia and had so much energy. She not only made the best American cheeseburgers I've ever tasted, but she inspired me to become educated by sharing her story. After having her seven children, her husband passed away, and because she had an education, she was able to raise all her children on her own as a university professor in the field of nursing. Another teacher and her husband were doctors who made significant achievements in the medical field here in Australia. These teachers inspired me to do my best in my education, with a goal to continue on to tertiary or university studies, which was my first goal!

Did you know that in a youth survey conducted by Mission Australia, approximately 96% of youth between the ages of 15-19 reported that the barriers about their future after school were academic ability, mental health and financial difficulty? The three personal concerns were mental stress, school and study and mental health while the most important issues for all youth nationwide were mental health, the environment; and equality and discrimination. (Mission Australia, 2019).

Do you remember having some of these concerns before graduating from school? Did you know what you could do to deal with these

Vision

barriers, concerns and issues? Do you have any suggestions to help young people deal with these concerns? Another topic was added to this survey, and the results were quite shocking in reference to bullying. Of 25,126 youth participants in the survey, 80% experienced bullying at school/TAFE/university, and 34% experienced bullying online.

Let me be bold and suggest that Spirit Freedom is and can be a solution for youth in relation to all these barriers, concerns and issues. By observing these issues through a spiritual perspective, we can overcome these challenges by striving for Spirit Freedom. Having a personal relationship with our Heavenly Father helped me to believe and be assured that when things didn't happen the way I wanted them to, they were not meant to happen. Our Heavenly Father always has a better plan for us when the time is right.

An example of this was when I set my mind on studying music when I graduated high school. I wasn't accepted into the university I had applied for, yet I was all right because another opportunity opened up so that I could work at the Commonwealth Bank to save up for my mission. I knew that our Heavenly Father always knew what was best for me. Regardless of the order, I knew that because I had a vision of what I wanted and asked our Heavenly Father for help to achieve it, somehow or another I had faith that all my goals would eventuate! Preparing for my mission was my next focus because it was clear to me that our Heavenly Father had a different plan for me, and that plan was sharing the gospel of Jesus Christ with others. Besides learning so much about money handling, accounts and customer service, over the next few years, I was able to save up for my mission. I also prepared spiritually by studying the scriptures, attending mission preparation classes, and everything else I could do to prepare before leaving for my mission at 21. The relationship I had with our Heavenly Father gave me peace and assurance that everything would work out as I continued to keep my end of the deal; keep his commandments and strived daily to be my best self!

I often wondered how many people knew that there was a Great Apostasy; a falling away from Jesus Christ's teachings and the church he organised. How many people knew that the priesthood authority was taken away after people fell into wickedness and the apostles that Jesus Christ chose were killed or exiled? How many people knew that the prophets in the Bible prophesied the Restoration of Jesus Christ's Church in 1830 because of the Great Apostasy? If they knew how crucial these events were, would it make a difference in the choices of which church they would join to receive eternal life? I believe that it definitely would make a difference! If people understood these events, being a member of The Church of Jesus Christ of Latter Day Saints would be the most important thing for them because it would give them every opportunity to return to their heavenly home and to be united with their heavenly parents! These thoughts motivated me to share these important truths with everyone even more!

Words from Acts when Peter and John spoke of the restoration of the Lord's church that would occur before His Second coming,

> **19** *Repent ye therefore, and be converted that your sins may be blotted out when the times of refreshing shall come from the presence of the Lord.*
> **20** *And he shall send Jesus Christ, which before was preached unto you.*
> **21** *Whom the heaven must receive until the times of restitution of all things, which God hath spoken by the mouth of all his holy prophets since the world began. (King James Version, Acts 3:19-21)*

Peter and John spoke of our time when prophets shall again be on the earth to lead the Lord's Church and kingdom on earth in The Church of Jesus Christ of Latter Day Saints. They continued to express the importance of listening to the prophets in our day,

> **24** *Yea, and all the prophets from Samuel and those that follow after, as many as have spoken, have likewise foretold of these days.*
> **25** *Ye are the children of the prophets, and of the covenant which God made with our fathers, saying unto Abraham, And in thy seed shall all the kindreds of the earth be blessed. (King James Version, Acts 3:24-25)*

Vision

My third goal was to travel the world, and especially to see the Seven Wonders of the World. My fourth goal was to be married for time and for all eternity in the Temple of the Lord, and, finally, my last goal was to be the best mother I could be for my children!

I believed that with our Heavenly Father, everything was possible, and I trusted that He would make my dreams come true as I continued to live His gospel!

The 15th prophet of this dispensation, President Gordon B. Hinkley expressed the impact of the restoration of the Gospel of Jesus Christ,

> *"That sublime occasion, the First Vision, parted the curtains through which came the restoration to earth of the Church of Christ. It came out of the wilderness of darkness, out of the bleakness of ages past into the glorious dawn of a new day. The Book of Mormon followed as another witness of the Lord Jesus Christ. His holy supernal priesthood was restored under the hands of those who held it anciently. Keys and powers were bestowed upon the Prophet and his associates. The ancient Church was again upon the earth with all of the blessings, powers, doctrines, keys, and principles of previous dispensations. It is [Christ's] Church. It carries His name. It is governed by His priesthood. There is no other name under heaven by which men must be saved. Joseph Smith ... became His great testator." (Hinckley, G. B., 2016)*

Without clear vision and hope of the future, we can be lost among the collateral of present chaos. In order to have clarity of vision and hope in life, I had to truly live the gospel of Jesus Christ. As mentioned in the earlier chapters, I had received my own personal confirmation through the Holy Ghost that the Book of Mormon was the word of God and that it was another testament along with the Holy Bible that Jesus is the Christ!

Knowing that the Book of Mormon is the word of God, then Joseph Smith, who translated this ancient record through the power of God, was His prophet! It wasn't until I left for my mission to the Adelaide Australia Mission that I received my own personal witness of this when I shared the First Vision story with other people in Joseph Smith's own words,

> *15 After I had retired to the place where I had previously designed to go, having looked around me, and finding myself alone, I kneeled down and began to offer up the desires of my heart to God. I had scarcely done so, when immediately I was seized upon by some power which entirely overcame me, and had such an astonishing influence over me as to bind my tongue so that I could not speak. Thick darkness gathered around me, and it seemed to me for a time as if I were doomed to sudden destruction.*
>
> *16 But, exerting all my powers to call upon God to deliver me out of the power of this enemy which had seized upon me, and at the very moment when I was ready to sink into despair and abandon myself to destruction—not to an imaginary ruin, but to the power of some actual being from the unseen world, who had such marvelous power as I had never before felt in any being—just at this moment of great alarm, I saw a pillar of light exactly over my head, above the brightness of the sun, which descended gradually until it fell upon me.*
>
> *17 It no sooner appeared than I found myself delivered from the enemy which held me bound. When the light rested upon me I saw two Personages whose brightness and glory defy all description, standing above me in the air. One of them spake unto me, calling me by name and said, pointing to the other—This is My Beloved Son. Hear Him!*
>
> *18 My object in going to inquire of the Lord was to know which of all the sects was right, that I might know which to join. No sooner, therefore, did I get possession of myself, so as to be able to speak, than I asked the Personages who stood above me in the light, which of all the sects was right (for at this time it had never entered into my heart that all were wrong)—and which I should join.*
>
> *19 I was answered that I must join none of them, for they were all wrong; and the Personage who addressed me said that all their creeds were an abomination in his sight; that those professors were*

all corrupt that: "they draw to me with their lips, but their hearts are far from me, they teach for doctrines the commandments of men, having a form of godliness, but they deny the power thereof." **20** *He again forbade me to join with any of them; and many other things did he say unto me, which I cannot write at this time. When I came to myself again, I found myself lying on my back, looking up into heaven. When the light had departed, I had no strength; but soon recovering in some degree, I went home. And as I leaned up to the fireplace, mother inquired what the matter was. I replied, "Never mind, all is well—I am well enough off." I then said to my mother, "I have learned for myself that Presbyterianism is not true." It seems as though the adversary was aware, at a very early period of my life, that I was destined to prove a disturber and an annoyer of his kingdom; else why should the powers of darkness combine against me? Why the opposition and persecution that arose against me, almost in my infancy? (Joseph Smith History 1:15-20)*

I had read this account several times in my family, church and seminary, but when sharing this with other people, it took on a whole new meaning! I felt the power of the Holy Ghost fill my heart and spirit! It pierced my soul, and I was humbled! It was another powerful and personal confirming of our Heavenly Father and Jesus Christ's unconditional love for all of us. This was a miracle, a marvellous work and a wonder.

I know that I shared this scripture earlier, but at 14 years old, Joseph Smith exercised incredible faith and courage after reading this verse to ask Heavenly Father for guidance as to which church or denomination to join at the time! By applying the concept of Faith, the miracle of the First Vision occurred!

"If any of you lack wisdom let him ask of God, that giveth to all men liberally, and upbraideth not; and it shall be given him." (King James Version, James 1:5)

Joseph Smith was instructed by Jesus Christ to restore His church to the earth and name it The Church of Jesus Christ of Latter Day Saints with prophets and apostles to lead and guide the members. There are now over 16 million members of the church worldwide. By volunteering our talents, time and resources, we are like a global international family helping each other, sharing our testimonies and giving more people the opportunity to accept Christ's teachings and his Gospel. I feel that everyone needs this feeling of belonging to a family greater than they can envision; and Jesus Christ's kingdom in the Church of Jesus Christ of Latter-day Saints.

If there is a specific path to return to our Heavenly Home, would you want to find it? I'm inviting you to find out for yourself if these things are true. By discovering it for yourself, you will be guided to enter the waters of baptism, receive the Gift of the Holy Ghost that Jesus Christ promises will assist in your life! By trusting in our Heavenly Father, He will mould you to become the best version of yourself! Jesus said,

"Be ye therefore perfect, even as your Father which is in heaven is perfect." (King James Version, Matthew 5:48)

Then after his resurrection when he appeared to the Nephites in the Americas (approx. 34 AD) he said to them,

"Therefore I would that ye should be perfect even as I, or your Father who is in heaven is perfect." (Book of Mormon, 3 Nephi 12:48)

Indicating that perfection can be attained through Jesus Christ's atonement and after we are all resurrected. Christ further explains that believing in Him is the path to eternal life,

"That whosoever believeth in him should not perish, but have eternal life." (King James Version, John 3:15)

Vision

In addition to what the Lord tells us in the Holy Bible during His living ministry among the Jews, he also shares these same truths with Nephi, who writes,

> **18** *And then are ye in this strait and narrow path which leads to eternal life; yea, ye have entered in by the gate; ye have done according to the commandments of the Father and the Son; and ye have received the Holy Ghost, which witness of the Father and the Son, unto the fulfilling of the promise which he hath made, that if ye entered in by the way ye should receive. (Book of Mormon, 2 Nephi 31:18)*

Paul, Jesus Christ's apostle in the New Testament, writes to the members of the church in Romans on how we can attain the gift of eternal life,

> "For the wages of sin is death; but the gift of God is eternal life through Jesus Christ our Lord." (King James Version, Romans 6:23)

Then in a revelation given to the prophet, Joseph Smith in 1829, the Lord speaks to all the people of the earth saying,

> "And, if you keep my commandments and endure to the end you shall have eternal life which is the greatest of all the gifts of God." (Doctrine and Covenants, Section 14:7)

I'm grateful and thankful for the First Vision that young 14-year-old Joseph Smith saw because it led to the marvellous work and a wonder of the Restoration of The Church of Jesus Christ of Latter Day Saints to the earth and the translation of the Book of Mormon through the power of God, our Heavenly Father who loves all His children and wants them to return to Him, when they choose.

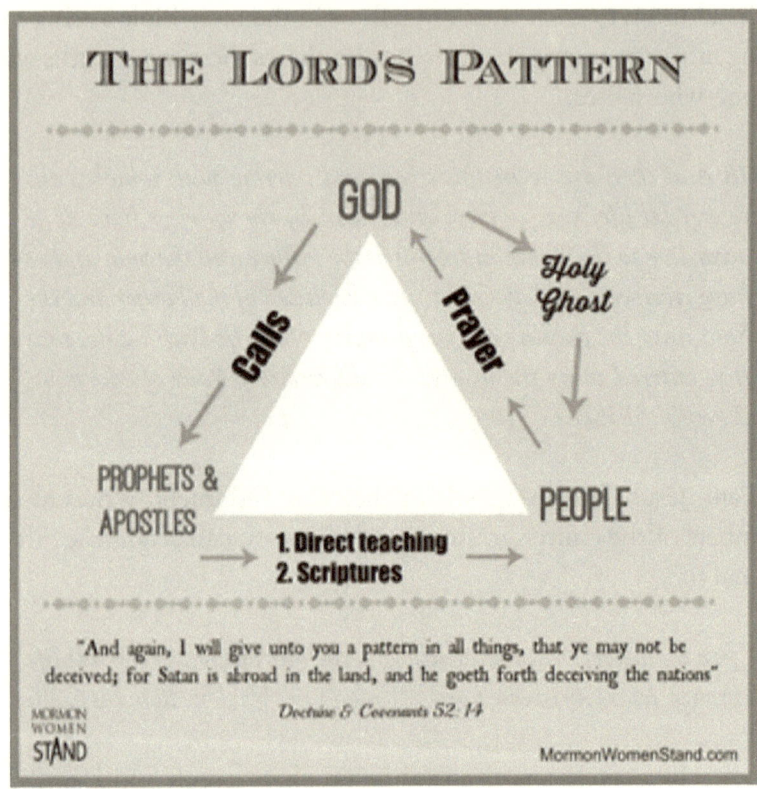

I'm grateful for the power of the Holy Ghost that testifies and teaches me that everything I've learned through the scriptures and heard from the prophets and those that love me are true.

Please take the opportunity to follow the next few steps:

1. Read the account of the First Vision, putting your-self in Joseph Smith's shoes as a young 14-year-old during the 1820s.
2. Pray to know that the First Vision and the Restoration of Jesus Christ's Church are true.
3. Take the time to listen to those positive feelings in your heart and positive thoughts that come to your mind, and then act on those feelings by joining The Church of Jesus Christ of Latter Day Saints with the ultimate promise of eternal life.

Vision

I promise that when you take the above steps with faith in the Lord, Jesus Christ and trusting in our Heavenly Father to answer your prayers, you will feel through the influence of the Holy Ghost that these things are true. It will change your life forever!

Here are some activities and strategies to further expand your imagination and vision for life!

1. Dream big and create a vision board of **8** things you would like to have in your life!
2. List 8 actions you can take towards those **8** things.
3. Follow through on those **8** actions daily.

My testimony that the young prophet Joseph Smith's spiritual experience, 'the First Vision' and later called by God to restore His true church on the earth once more strengthens daily, allowing the spirit of revelation to work in my life.

- Taloa Walters

CHAPTER 8

Discover

Men and women

who turn their lives over to **God**

will discover that He can make a lot more

OUT OF THEIR LIVES THAN THEY CAN.

-Ezra Taft Benson

We are all unique, different, special, beautiful, and have the ability to discover our specific needs, talents, character, interests, personality, and develop who we truly are with the help of our Heavenly Father, Jesus Christ and the Holy Ghost! In this chapter, you will understand how we are to be refined through personal sacrifice of time, effort and worldly desires to discover the power within us to overcome trials and afflictions in life. You will realise your inner strength that comes from drawing on the powers of Heaven and treasure who you are!

Another prophet of this dispensation, and the ninth President of The Church of Jesus Christ of Latter Day Saints, President David O McKay said,

> *"Man is a spiritual being, a soul, and at some point of his life everyone is possessed with an irresistible desire to know his relationship to the infinite. There is something within him which urges him to rise above himself, to control his environment, to master the body and all things physical and live in a higher, more beautiful world." (Eyring, H. B., 2007).*

The current General Relief Society Presidency of the Church of Jesus Christ of Latter Day Saints, Sister Jean B. Bingham (President), Sister Sharon Eubank (1st counsellor), and Sister Reyna I. Aburto (2nd counsellor) are an inspiration to me and examples of women of faith, courage, charity and service. In the Relief Society Declaration described above, we can be guided in our responsibilities within our homes and within our communities how we may service and in so doing achieve self-discovery.

Lack of identity breeds mediocrity and unrealised potential. Our identity as spiritual children of God motivates personal development, self-mastery and unconditional service, understanding that with God, we can accomplish, achieve and attain anything.

I was blessed with opportunities to teach at church. Can you imagine being a teacher to women who had a whole lifetime of experiences? It was quite humbling, and the most wonderful thing about it was that I learned so much about their lives, which ultimately strengthened my faith. It became quite clear that by living the Gospel, I became the vessel in which the spirit could touch the hearts of the women in my class. I discovered that the same process the Holy Ghost helped me with - learning to play the organ growing up, being effective in several church assignments or callings, developing skills in the workplace and being an effective missionary for the Church - applied to everything!

I was thrilled to serve the Lord and to share the Gospel among the people in the Australia Adelaide Mission! I was even reunited with my

Discover

THE RELIEF SOCIETY DECLARATION

We are beloved spirit daughters of God,
and our lives have meaning, purpose, and direction.
As a worldwide sisterhood, we are united in our devotion
to Jesus Christ, our Savior and Exemplar.
We are women of faith, virtue, vision, and charity who:

Increase our testimonies of Jesus Christ
through prayer and scripture study.

Seek spiritual strength by following the
promptings of the Holy Ghost.

Dedicate ourselves to strengthening
marriages, families, and homes.

Find nobility in motherhood
and joy in womanhood.

Delight in service and good works.

Love life and learning.

Stand for truth and righteousness.

Sustain the priesthood
as the authority of God on earth.

Rejoice in the blessings of the temple,
understand our divine destiny,
and strive for exaltation.

(LDS, 2000)

cousin, Rubina, who was an incredible example of faith, love and talent to me! I've always believed that there are no coincidences and that Heavenly Father has a better plan for us than we have for ourselves. My mission parents, President and Sister Weston, were wonderful examples to me of love and devotion to the Lord. They embraced over 100 missionaries ages 19+ with encouragement, passion, motivation, support, generosity, kindness and Christlike love! They travelled from the USA with their family to serve the Lord in missionary service. I loved serving the people in the Australia Adelaide Mission! Over the next 18 months, I grew spiritually, intellectually and socially. I was extremely quiet at the beginning of my mission, but by the time I left the mission field, I was much more confident, bold and driven! A lesson that was reinforced more on my mission was that complete submission to our Heavenly Father's will was the only way to live. He did more for me during that time than I could have ever imagined achieving on my own. Trust me, I had many challenges, rejections, and was even chased by dogs on my bike, yet I discovered more about myself and developed an even closer relationship with our Heavenly Father and Jesus Christ!

I had the privilege of working with amazing missionaries from all over the United States, Australia and the Pacific who shared the same love for our Heavenly Father and Jesus Christ as well as a desire to share the gospel with the people of Australia. Although there were challenges each day, the blessing of meeting people who were willing to learn about the gospel made it all worthwhile. I had the blessing of travelling to Darwin and serving the people there for approximately four months. During my time there, we shared the gospel with many Aboriginal people and connected with them spiritually. Seeing families accept the gospel of Jesus Christ, being baptised and experiencing the joy, peace, comfort, and the love of our Heavenly Father and Jesus Christ through the Holy Ghost brought so much happiness to me.

My mission taught me that no matter the circumstances and situations in life, when sharing the gospel of Jesus Christ, it's the spirit of the work that counts. It's the influence and power of the Holy Ghost that touches a heart and changes lives.

Discover

We are all unique, different and possess through the influence of the Holy Ghost many gifts, all for the benefit of serving others and helping them come to know our Heavenly Father. I believe that through inspiration many throughout time and history have received personal revelation using many different forms of communication accessing the power of the Holy Ghost to connect with our Heavenly Father, Jesus Christ and the Spirit. Heavenly Father allows us to receive knowledge according to our desires for our benefit and for the benefit of all his spirit children. Through personal experiences, I have found that through applied kinesiology, and energy healing, the same processes of Faith and trust in our Heavenly Father are applied! Many people have been able to access knowledge and understanding of their abilities, talents, gifts and intuition through sincere prayer and listening to the Holy Ghost. This, I believe, is the same process of receiving personal revelation from our Heavenly Father which leads to success in life and to achieve Spirit Freedom!

To develop this process of personal revelation for self-discovery, I encourage you to:

1. Pray to be guided to the people who exemplify faith, love and trust in God for personal learning and development.
2. Apply the attitude of service daily.
3. Share the lessons you have learned with others.

A few strategies to strengthen this connection to your spirit:

1. Surround yourself with like-minded people of Faith.
2. Learn techniques of applied kinesiology relating to muscle testing to discover generational influences that may be connected to physical, mental or emotional blockages/
3. Clear these blockages using affirmations, essential oils, natural elements or natural materials relating to energy healing.

Taloa Walters

I am a child of God, inheriting from him the ability to overcome all things through his miraculous power and love. He loves me and knows me by name. Through His spirit, I can access all knowledge to heal physically, mentally, emotionally and spiritually. He understands me better than anyone and promises to help me ultimately become the child He wants me to be.

-Taloa Walters

Discover

My Mission

CHAPTER 9

Reflect

You have come from His presence to live on this earth for a season,

to reflect the Savior's love and teachings,

and to bravely let your light shine for all to see.

-Thomas S. Monson

We can learn more than we can comprehend through reflection and remembering lessons, experiences and knowledge gained along the way, drawing strength from them to keep going. When we apply reflection daily, we grow in wisdom, strengthen our minds, build resilience, and discover the formula for mental health and the path to pure joy.

British author, David Amerland said,

> "According to neuroscience, self-reflection is theorised as to occupy as much as 50% of our waking life.... Self-reflection allows us to time-travel inside our head. It reinforces memories that form

part of our sense of identity; it aids in long-term planning and goals and plays a key role in creativity." (Amerland, D. 2019).

Another church leader Erich W Kopischke explained that,

"First, we need to know that our hearts are honest and broken. How do we know that? We begin by engaging in sincere self-reflection. The heart is the center of our feelings. As we look into our hearts, we screen ourselves. What no one around us knows, we surely know. We know our motives and desires. When we engage in sincere, honest reflection, we do not rationalize or deceive ourselves." (Kopischke, E. W., 2013).

When we lack self-reflection, we lack effective learning. Mental health motivates physical health and reflects spiritual strength.

Returning from my mission in 1994 was quite a transition and reflection of the year and a half devoted to serving our Heavenly Father and sharing the gospel of Jesus Christ with the citizens of Adelaide and the Northern Territory. My time there strengthened my love of the people and of our Heavenly Father as I witnessed the power of the Atonement in my life and in the lives of those who accepted the Gospel through my efforts.

With my spiritual experiences on the mission field coupled with my spiritual childhood experiences, I felt the power of the Holy Ghost constantly in my life strengthening my mind and body through service and connecting with others to gain wisdom from their life experiences. One of the most important lessons I learned on my mission is that everyone is a valued member in society, community and in our Heavenly Father's family. We all learn from each other and contribute to making life the best experience we can. Trusting in our Heavenly Father, who is the source of all knowledge, putting forth our best efforts in all learning and serving others by sharing the knowledge we have gained in our journeys.

Ultimately, the strongest connection to our Heavenly Father comes as we tap into our capabilities to draw on the powers of heaven! The

Reflect

focus on mental exertion was explicit, and the flow of energy in spiritual communication of pure knowledge phenomenally changed my life.

A quote that impressed me by Patricia T Holland was,

"We must have courage to be imperfect while striving for perfection." (Holland, P. T., 1987)

President Weston encouraged me to apply to university at my last missionary interview, which impacted my life and is something I will always be grateful to him for. Returning home from Adelaide, I contacted the church university liaison representative who advised I apply to Brigham Young University, Hawaii Campus as they had a return missionary scholarship that would pay for my entire tuition fee. As music had become an incredible part of most of my life serving in the church, I applied for the instrumental music program specialising in the organ. I had faith that everything would work out according to the Lord's will! I was accepted and would start at the beginning of 1995!

Before I left for university, my mum, sister Sarai and I travelled to Samoa to visit with my grandma, Tina, who was extremely ill and could not walk. It was heartbreaking to see her so physically weak, yet her spirit was strong. The only comfort I felt was that she had eventually joined the church when I was 16 years old in 1987 after reading the Book of Mormon. I knew stronger than ever that whatever would happen to her, we would see each other again and live together forever after death. Two weeks after returning to Australia from Samoa, she passed away. It was difficult not going back for her funeral, but the gospel and the knowledge of the Eternal Plan of Happiness gave me hope, comfort, and peace!

My heart filled with gratitude for my Brigham Young University Hawaii (BYUH) experience, as it was nothing short of a miracle, and the hand of the Lord in my life was even more evident with the fulfilment of my first goal to further my education! I learned from amazing professors and the friendships I developed, particularly a dear friend, Lani and her family who cared for me when I first arrived, the knowledge that I attained, the memorable experiences I had and the spiritual strength I received, were definitely miracles! I love and cherish all my friendships that were built during that time, as they added even more to the discovery of who I truly was! I learned to build on everything I had gained from my mission and was humbled in the additional life lessons that took place during my Brigham Young University Hawaii life. I had the incredible opportunity to serve in the Church on the university campus that embraced everything I believed in. I felt enriched, wealthy, and complete in so many ways, but most of all, I felt the constant power of the Holy Ghost and the love of our Heavenly Father! I was blessed to also work at the Polynesian Cultural Center (PCC), Hawaii's top tourist attraction and to be surrounded with talented, devoted and hardworking members of The Church of Jesus Christ of Latter Day Saints in sharing the Polynesian culture with the world. I felt the passion and developed a deeper love for my culture and other Polynesian cultures. From my boss, Tali, who was an amazing secretary to Newell and Logo, I learned how the beauty of hard work, devotion and dedication to a vision through music, song and dance could touch and change lives! I had the blessing to travel to China in the summer of 1997 as part of the PCC promotional team for two months. Our promotional director, Delsa, and team leader David were extraordinary and incredibly patient with me during my learning process. Physically, I worked harder than I'd ever done before to prepare for the trip. It had been the first time they had considered a team of international students to travel and promote the PCC internationally, and to be selected was a dream! They knew nothing of my third goal as a teenager, which was to travel the world and see the wonders of the world before marriage, yet our Heavenly Father knew, and that's what mattered most. Our trip to Shenzhen, China and working in 'The Windows of the World', a world cultural centre, for two months teaching the Chinese employees the Polynesian cultural music, song and dances is a source of great faith, strength, joy, hard work, endurance and service to me. The experiences there were beyond my imagination of travelling the world; the Republic of China built miniature models of all the wonders of the world in one place. During our breaks from practice and performance shows, we would climb the miniature Eiffel Tower, walk the miniature Sahara Desert, sit on a real

Reflect

camel, admire the Pyramid of Giza, walk through the miniature Taj Mahal, fascinated by the intricacy of the coloured glass in the structure, walk the miniature Great Wall of China, admire the miniature Grand Canyon, miniature Colosseum, an American Indian reserve, miniature of Amsterdam, Holland, the Leaning Tower of Pisa and the miniature PCC where we worked. These were remarkable highlights and memories I treasure. I also had the unfortunate opportunity to visit a hospital because I caught pneumonia while we were there.

It was at Brigham Young University where I met my future eternal companion, Aaron, the year before in 1996. We started dating in February 1997 after a Valentine's Ball, were engaged on March 8 in the Hawaii Temple, and after my China trip we travelled to Australia and were married in the Sydney Australia Temple on December 27, 1997, just after Christmas. My younger sister, Si'i and the rest of my siblings helped to plan and organise our wedding, which was beautiful and more extravagant than I'd ever imagined. We flew into Sydney, Australia a few days before Christmas, married a couple of days after and rushed back to Hawaii to continue school. It was a whirlwind of a wedding but definitely worth it! I'll always be grateful to my sister Si'i, all my siblings, my parents, and my whole family, including my in-laws for that wonderful and memorable week!

I had amazing Bishops and mentors at BYUH. Bishop Freebairn, Bishop Winget Bishop Akoi, and Bishop Tew and their families played significant roles in our lives at the time. We love them dearly and treasure all they did for our family!

The Lord works in mysterious ways! I graduated from Brigham Young University with an Associate Degree in Music – Instrumental and a Bachelor Degree in Science, Special Education (SPED) in June 2000. Aaron graduated with a Bachelor Degree in Business, Hospitality and Tourism in December 2000. The following year, Aaron and I welcomed our daughter, Siona. A couple of years later on Valentine's Day 2003, Tiara joined our small family. Then Kirra arrived, sharing her birthday with her dad, 30 years later on the same day. Finally, our last daughter Elena was born in 2007 in Tweed Heads, Australia. I'm truly grateful for the blessing of my beautiful daughters in my life and thank our Heavenly

Father for them each day! They have been miracles, blessings, inspirational examples and an incredible strength to me over the last 19 years.

Reflection is something we naturally do - sometimes consciously and sometimes subconsciously. Focusing on it helps us understand the lessons we are meant to learn and how it can be applied to other situations in our lives. It's all for our benefit, growth and development!

It takes conscious effort and a decision to reflect, and it involves processes of noting down the experience and lesson learned from it – asking yourself how it can be applied to this situation. Recording our reflections in journals helps with recollection and also allows our children or loved ones to understand our feelings, thoughts and perceptions during those specific experiences. Sometimes after reflections we come to understand who we are or who we have become over time, through the life lessons we have learned and especially in the experiences we have had throughout our lives.

Ask yourself, are you happy? Are you satisfied with your life? If you are, that's incredible, but if you're not, ask yourself, was there any other time in my life where I was happy? Think about that and write it down. What were you doing then that made you happy that you're not doing now? Writing it down can help you discover where to begin.

To begin to reflect on your life, follow these steps:
1. Self-reflect daily through prayer, meditation and journaling.
2. Practise mental exercises using positive memories to manifest positive feelings.
3. Reflect on the last 5-9 years and set goals of what you want to improve, achieve and attract into your life in the next 5-9 years!

Self-reflection is the conscious effort to make sense of personal revelation we receive from our Heavenly Father during our lifetime on earth! Reflections on life's experiences and feedback from people we respect, love, connect with or are mentored by should be treasured on this extraordinary journey returning to our heavenly home.

-Taloa Walters

Reflect

Taloa Walters

CHAPTER 10

Endure

There is nothing that we are enduring that

Jesus does not understand.

-Robert. D. Hales

We can commit to our Heavenly Father and ourselves to keep on the path of goodness, service, and honesty to live the best life we are meant to live. In this chapter, you will come to understand that through exact obedience to the promptings of the Holy Ghost, you will feel the assurance of promised blessings and continue to witness miracles daily in your life. By relishing in those miracles and happy moments, you will have hope in a glorious future and recommit wholeheartedly each day to our Heavenly Father, feeling his love and growing in His knowledge, in His light and in His power.

To endure in anything, you need to have commitment! What is commitment? In a 2010 blog by Todd Smith, a successful entrepreneur and founder of Little Things Matter, he shares the wisdom that commitment is,

"A binding pledge that obligates you to assume a position or carry out a course of action. Making a commitment to what you do – whether in your personal life or your professional life – is one of the most fundamental principles of success." (Smith, T., 2010)

Furthermore, Anthony Mendes describes the four cornerstones of commitment in his book, Inspiring Commitment: How to Win Employee Loyalty in Chaotic Times,

1. Vision – The ability to visualise success. Without a vision it is very difficult to make commitment work.
2. Insight – The ability to know yourself and apply this self-knowledge to the commitment process.
3. Acceptance of change – The ability to accept change and to focus on the things you can control.
4. Integration – Combining your values, thoughts, words and actions into the commitment process. (Mendes, A. 1996)

One of the apostles, Elder Wirthlin, who is dear to my heart and who spoke at my BYUH graduation in June 2000, gave some powerful advice,

"Living the gospel does not mean the storms of life will pass us by, but we will be better prepared to face them with serenity and peace. 'Search diligently, pray always, and be, believing,' the Lord admonished, 'and all things shall work together for your good, if ye walk uprightly.'" (Wirthlin, J. B., 2000).

Without endurance, there is no commitment, and when there is no commitment on our part, endurance cannot exist. Endure or endurance, also related to tolerance, resilience, character, courage, and self-assurance; is one's ability to apply oneself and maintain sustainability for a long period of time, also having the ability to resist, recover from, or obtain freedom from trauma, wounds, or exhaustion.

I found that when I committed to going on my mission, no matter how difficult situations were, I persisted because I made a commitment because of the tender mercies and unconditional love I felt from our Heavenly Father. There were many opportunities to quit and give up because at times things were difficult; abuse from Atheists, Anti-Christs, Anti-Christians or people who didn't want to listen to our message, didn't understand the message we shared or felt threatened by us. These experiences often brought doubt even questioning why I was on a mission, yet through daily prayer to our Heavenly Father, I was reminded of the joy, peace, comfort and love I felt through the power of the Holy Ghost! My commitment to serve our Heavenly Father was an expression of gratitude for all He had done for me. It was through endurance on my mission that I discovered inner spiritual, mental and physical strength and a deeper faith, love for people and passion for service.

Endurance in my studies at BYUH even after trials, challenges and afflictions that occurred in student teaching, relationships and church commitments, prepared me for the strength I would need when facing thyroid cancer in 2012 and witnessing my sister Sarai pass away from breast cancer in April 2015. The following year, in 2016, my sister-in-law, Melissa passed away from breast cancer in August, and my sister-in-law, Susana passed away from renal failure at the end of the year, around Christmas. I recently lost another sister in law, Julie, in May 2020. I love them all so much and cherish memories we shared together! My knowledge of the gospel of Jesus Christ comforts me because I know that I will see them again after this life.

Through the strength of the Lord and the power of the Holy Ghost, our Heavenly Father helped me physically and spiritually watch over my sister's children, my four nieces and two nephews, for a period of time. My nieces and nephews are now with their father, which is fantastic. I love them with all my heart, and although there were challenges because each of them mourned the loss of their mother in different ways, I found I relied even more on our Heavenly Father for guidance. I believed that our Heavenly Father and Jesus Christ would make up the difference of what I couldn't do. During that time, I was able to fulfil another goal and received my Masters of Education, Early Childhood Education and Care, in the field of research, graduating in 2019.

Miracles have never ceased to happen in my life because of the marvellous and unconditional love of our Heavenly Father! We can achieve all we desire to accomplish when we understand that it is in His time because he knows best! I believe that Heavenly Father can create, refine, or magnify our abilities and lives more than we can on our own. As I searched for ways to help my nieces, nephews and daughters deal with the loss of their mother and aunties, I was guided by the Holy Ghost to connect with friends, Cassile and Tanya who introduced me to applied kinesiology where I learned techniques and used muscle testing to discover emotional issues all the children were dealing with daily, then using affirmations, essential oils and energy clearing to help them overcome these issues. I was also led to other friends Priscilla and Reihana who introduced me to Reiki and energy healing techniques. I believe that through the Holy Ghost and with an open mind I was able to use these specific techniques channelling Faith to help all ten children deal with loss and emotional struggles each day. I believed that learning these strategies through the power of the Holy Ghost truly helped me to deal with every occasion that would arise. The flow of positive energy in our home many times was a miracle to me. Teaching early morning religion classes to teenagers helped us focus on the spiritual aspect of life, which gave me physical and spiritual strength from day to day! Always praying together and having Jesus Christ the centre of our home made a huge difference. Remaining anxiously engaged in a good cause and optimistic in times of challenges, maintaining focus, and ultimately living the gospel the best I could, a day at a time, our Heavenly Father provided the strength for me to endure in caring and protecting my family as well as achieving my own personal goals. Serving in the church as a seminary teacher was life-saving for me in every way possible. I was able to start and end the day focused on our Heavenly Father, his love and will for me, trusting in Him and doing my part, exerting all energy to face all daily issues, challenges and relying on His help to guide me through the power of the Holy Ghost. I felt more gratitude and experienced more miracles than I could even write about and witnessed His hand in my life daily.

Endure

I feel the power of His love even as I write this book with the hope and prayer that as you read these pages, you may feel His amazing love for you.

Endure is such a power-filled word that means so much more to me than words can describe. Enduring to the end also means to commit to finding the truth, discovering your path and continuing on your journey with our Heavenly Father's help to return to our Heavenly Home with the ultimate promise of never-ending hope, love, joy, peace, comfort, and happiness beyond our imagination!

Sometimes it's human nature to fall, resort to old habits and make mistakes but there is always hope through Jesus Christ to repent, to return, to invite goodness and love into our lives and get back on track. If you're wondering how to keep going, the best way to endure, stay true, and keep on the path is to have the end in mind. Eternal love, peace, comfort, joy, and happiness are awaiting us, and all we need to do is to endure to the end in Faith!

Trust me, there have been many times where I've lost focus or felt like giving up because life's challenges seemed too much to bear. As soon as those moments happen, I get on my knees and pray for help. I take the time to listen to the Holy Ghost, paying attention to the positive feelings and thoughts in my mind. Once I do this, I feel gratitude for all I've been blessed with and begin focusing on the end in my mind – Eternal Life. One of the most important lessons I've learned so far is to take a day at a time and even moments at a time. Relish in the happy moments of achievement! Encourage children to do the same by being the best example of happiness! Remember, success takes gradual effort, and it is up to you to achieve it. Believe me, you can!

To maintain optimism, gratitude and invite the light and love of our Heavenly Father into your life daily, here are some strategies you can apply:

1. As soon as you wake, stand by your bed, raise your arms as high as you can then close your eyes and visualise the brightest light you can imagine above your head. Pretend you have this amazing light in the grasp of your hands moving this light

down through your body slowly from the top of your head, lighting up your whole body until you get to your feet!
2. Fall to your knees and pour out your heart to your Heavenly Father. Be free in all your expressions and aspirations for the day ahead!
3. Finally, visualise yourself at the end of the day happy that you've accomplished all you set out to do! Remember that feeling and get excited! This feeling will help you get through the day!
4. Remember to be happy in the moment no matter what happens and relish the journey by expressing gratitude, positivity and love!

'Endure to the end' is knowledge that the Gospel of Jesus Christ is true and choosing to have Faith in Him each day no matter what happens.

-Taloa Walters

Endure

CHAPTER 11

Be Creative

Creative expression can also represent the celebration

of our gratitude to God for our gifts and talents.

-Neal. A. Maxwell

We each have a voice and can learn to express ourselves by communicating our feelings, thoughts and insights to connect to Heavenly Father and everyone! I hope this chapter can help you discover your voice by understanding your divine identity through the power of the Holy Ghost. You may be able to channel this power to develop emotional intelligence, and through effective expression of your voice achieve success in all relationships. Understanding that expression is essential, crucial, and lifesaving will help you achieve ultimate happiness and success throughout your life!

Did you know that there are approximately 800,000 suicides every year worldwide? According to the World Health Organization, the statistics show that one person dies every 40 seconds! Suicide is the second worldwide leading cause of death in young people ages 15-29 - next to the first leading cause of death being vehicle accidents. Mental illness has been a worldwide issue that global countries and governments have been battling over the last couple of years due to the increase of cases often leading to suicides. (WHO, 2020). There is so much we can do individually to assist in suicide prevention.

Regarding suicide victims, parents who have lost children through suicide and anyone affected by it, Sister McConkie said,

"....the redemptive power of the Atonement to heal all that isn't right in this life, to correct all that isn't fair in this life." (McConkie, C. F., 2018)

She continues to say,

"As we seek to increase faith, as we seek to do things that invite the Holy Ghost, the comforter, the comforter is real and the peace does come." (McConkie, C. F., 2018)

It is so important to express our voice in a non-judgmental approach, and it's only through the Holy Ghost that the expression of our thoughts, actions and words are received in the precise spirit it is relayed in our society, community and the world we live in.

President Gordon B. Hinckley also expressed that,

"Our lives are the only meaningful expression of what we believe and in whom we believe. And the only real wealth, for any of us, lies in our faith." (Hinckley, G. B., 2017)

If we silence our voice, our relationships and connections to our Heavenly Father and others are non-existent. We can find ourselves in mental darkness that can lead to drastic actions, suicidal thoughts and loneliness. Expression of our feelings, thoughts and words free us from these mental dark moments of despair, depression, and burdens.

Voice

It was the lack of expression that led to the feeling that I was a burden to my family for what had happened to me as a child and feeling that suicide was the last resort.

My desperate expression of prayer to my Heavenly Father opened the floodgates of love, hope, light and peace, changing the course of my life forever. Things could have taken a different course in those short moments of darkness or mindset of hopelessness, despair and no escape. I am eternally grateful for our Heavenly Father's love that engulfed my whole body, giving me hope and lifting me out of the pitfall of death and suicide I had gradually allowed myself to fall into. My seven-year-old expression of help to our Heavenly Father was answered immediately and was the beginning of many prayers and communications with Him! Worthy music and devoted service in The Church of Jesus Christ of Latter Day Saints as an organist was my way of expressing gratitude and love to our Heavenly Father and everyone else.

Expressing our voice is essential to living a full and complete life. Our voice needs to be heard because it's the essence of connection and can strengthen bonds in relationship with our Heavenly Father and everyone. Life ology, psychology and other mental health experts and professionals all agree that "When it comes to happiness and success in life, emotional intelligence matters just as much as intellectual ability." (Miles, M., 2020). According to the Oxford Learner's Dictionaries, the definition of emotional intelligence is the ability and capability of expressing emotions with control, awareness and handles interpersonal relationships with empathy, sensitivity and good judgment (Oxford Learner's Dictionaries, 2020).

I learned the importance of communicating with our Heavenly Father, pouring out my heart to him in every situation, understanding that He was the source of all my blessings and miracles! Realising that our Heavenly Father existed and loved me was the beginning of a spiritual journey filled with happy, sad, challenging, heartbreaking, hopeful, joyful, peaceful and loving moments. My journey of discovering my voice has gradually developed over the years, where I had the courage to share my feelings, thoughts, beliefs and values verbally and through acts of service!

This journey has led me to have the courage to share my story, and although I've only shared a small part of my life with you, doing so is an expression of my love, gratitude, devotion and respect for our Heavenly Father, our older brother, Jesus Christ and the powerful gift of the Holy Ghost for the strength that they have blessed me throughout my life.

By finding my voice and sharing my story, I hope that you will feel our Heavenly Father's love for you and for all His spirit children on the earth today. I have the purest of intention and only desire the very best for you in your life.

We all have stories to tell, and I encourage you to share your story with the intention to uplift and strengthen the human spirit, encouraging each individual to reach their potential. Heavenly Father knows us all; He knows our hearts, intentions and thoughts. Our stories will be unique because we are each exceptional even before the very foundation of the world!

Understand who you are, a unique daughter or son of our Heavenly Father and that you are of incredible worth and value to Him. Know that His unconditional love for you gives Him the ultimate power to assist you on your return journey home. With each step towards Him you will grow in knowledge, and with every righteous choice you make, He promises exaltation and eternal life, the greatest of all his gifts to all His spirit children. Remembering Him and feeling His absolute love daily will give you courage to share your own journey to strengthen others.

Three things I would encourage you to practise applying into your life to discover and express your voice:

1. Ask our Heavenly Father for guidance and courage to express your voice daily regarding your faith, life and truth.
2. Develop emotional intelligence daily by being open to others and allow yourself to be vulnerable without fear! Understand that positivity, empathy, sensitivity and good judgment are valuable attributes to possess.
3. Expressing your voice allows more miracles to flow into your life because of your gratitude, patience, and pure love.

Voice

Expressing our voice in words and deeds reflects our faith, life and truth.

-Taloa Walters

CHAPTER 12

Be believing, be happy, don't get discouraged.

Things will work out.

-Gordon B. Hinckley

We have the ability to influence, empower and impact others for good, as we truly submit to our Heavenly Father's will, trust in Him and live the gospel. You possess the power within you to inspire others, and you will come to understand that you were chosen to live on the earth at this precise moment in time. As you listen and submit your will to our Heavenly Father, listening and acting upon the promptings of the Holy Ghost, you will increase in courage and develop trustworthiness to influence many lives! You can become an instrument in our Heavenly Father's hands in bringing joy, happiness, and peace to all his spirit children through all generations of time, blessing all who come in contact with you because they will feel our Heavenly Father's love for them through your words, thoughts and actions.

Striving to be the best you can be inspires others to do the same! John Quincy Adams said,

"If your actions inspire others to dream more, learn more, do more and become more, you are a leader." (Luttrell, M., 2020).

It is inevitable to become a great leader when you become your best self and put our Heavenly Father's will first and foremost! He knows you better than you know yourself and knows what you are capable of becoming. Service is the ultimate way you can inspire others. It's important to pray for inspiration and listen for personal revelation from our Heavenly Father and Jesus Christ through the power of the Holy Ghost. Reflecting on the miracles throughout your life and having the courage to share this with others, inspire them to do the same. President Russell M. Nelson is a wonderful example of how being educated as a surgeon gave him the opportunity to become a founder of the first heart pump, which allowed for the first heart transplant. He said,

"Education is the difference between wishing you could help other people and being able to help them." (Nelson, R. M., 2014).

He inspired me to pursue education because it increased my capacity to serve others. Another wonderful example to me of service is President Gordon B. Hinckley, who expressed that,

"Generally speaking, the most miserable people I know are those who are obsessed with themselves; the happiest people I know are those who lose themselves in the service of others...By and large, I have come to see that if we complain about life, it is because we are thinking only of ourselves." (Hinckley, G. B., 2020)

Each of us has the ability to inspire those around us as we pursue our interests with the purpose of helping other people. As a piano teacher, my goal is to inspire my students to achieve their goals of proficiency as pianists, growing from milestone to milestone! I also encourage them to build a relationship with our Heavenly Father and Jesus Christ through music, reminding them that "with God all things are possible." As I mentioned earlier, worthy music assisted me to connect with our Heavenly Father through the power of the Holy Ghost. Through music, I felt healing power and inspired love, hope, and peace! Christ's teachings strengthened me throughout my childhood, teenage years and my adult life.

I know that our Heavenly Father, Jesus Christ and the Holy Ghost can help you through difficult challenges, trials and afflictions in your life because of the experiences I have had in my life. My whole life is evidence that the Godhead exists and has purpose! That purpose is for all mankind to return to their presence in the Celestial Kingdom!

Inspiration, personal insights, revelation and inner peace are available to each person who desires these things. Worthy music inspires our spirits to connect with the source of all knowledge, our Heavenly Father but also to connect with each other and the world we live in.

Did you know that music and sound waves affect the growth of plants? In an article written by Meg Michelle, she states that music and sound waves help plants physically grow in the same way they help humans grow emotionally, mentally, socially and physically. Sound waves communicate messages through 'mechanoreceptors' that plants possess, respond to and can act as a defence impacting growth. We have those same 'mechanoreceptors' in our ears which affect our responses to situations, warnings, and communication when listening to music or sound waves (Michelle, M. 2020).

I am blessed to currently serve as a counsellor to my sister, Sii who is the president of the Camden Ward Primary, where we are responsible for the spiritual welfare of children from 18 months to 10 years of age. We have the privilege of serving our Heavenly Father in teaching Christ's doctrine to over 60 children. For me, it is a huge blessing to work together with teachers and other leaders to help each child understand the Saviour's teachings and feel His love for them through his atoning sacrifice! Jesus Christ's personal invitation to 'Come Follow Me' extended to all is a spiritual educational program inspired by our Heavenly Father through general church leaders of The Church of Jesus Christ of Latter Day Saints. The joy I've been able to receive in getting to know each child has given me insight in a microscopic way to comprehend the tremendous love our Heavenly Father has for each child in our care.

Also, in another area of service in the Church of Jesus Christ of Latter Day Saints, I am blessed to have the opportunity to teach youth within the Seminary program, which is a morning scripture study class from 6-7am from Monday to Thursday. I teach approximately 14-17 teenagers in years 9-12 attending several different high schools in the area. This class gives teenagers an opportunity to draw closer to their Heavenly Father and Saviour, Jesus Christ through the power of the Holy Ghost each morning to assist them in daily life. By the time they graduate from high school, they will also graduate from the Seminary program with a four-year diploma in religious education studying The Holy Bible – Old Testament (1st year), The Holy Bible – New Testament (2nd year), Book of Mormon (3rd year), and Doctrine and Covenants/Pearl of Great Price (4th year). This year because of the COVID-19 pandemic we have had class on Zoom. My desire to inspire youth to strengthen their personal relationships with our Heavenly Father and Jesus Christ and follow Christ's example found in the scriptures is one of my passions because I've experienced it myself in my youth.

We inspire others around us all the time. It's the natural result of living the best life we can. Each goal we achieve in life inspires everyone around us. Our thoughts, words and deeds can inspire others when we are mindful of using them to promote positivity, kindness and love. This is the power to inspire. We all have it within us!

Inspiring others is crucial in the world we live in today. The more good we do, the more we inspire others to do the same. Each topic in my book can help someone at any stage on their spiritual journey in life. The topics in each chapter are not meant to follow in sequence, but each topic stands on its own, and although I've shared many personal experiences at different times of my life sequentially it's not an indication that you will follow suit. The importance of 'inspire' is

Inspire

that we each have the potential to be leaders in our lives, among our families and friends. We have within us the power to inspire, and it's up to us to express it!

Recently the Holy Ghost has led me to an opportunity which fulfils a dream and goal I've had for a while to attain financial freedom in order to help as many of our Heavenly Father's spirit children achieve their dreams along the way! All blessings in my life are accredited to our loving Heavenly Father.

I'm reminded of a scripture which says,

> "But seek ye first the kingdom of God and his righteousness, and all these things shall be added unto you." (Book of Mormon, 3 Nephi 13:33)

I truly believe that in attaining Spirit Freedom, and by spiritually preparing for the future, our Heavenly Father will bless us to be able to provide for our needs and assist others to do the same according to our righteous desires. (If you're interested in further details relating to this, please refer to my offers and website in the back of my book).

The following strategies can help you to know how you can inspire others in your life:

1. Pray for opportunities to serve others daily.
2. Listen for personal revelation as to who you can help each day.
3. Inspire others by humbly sharing your experiences and miracles of service daily, acknowledging the hand of the Lord in all your blessings!

If you follow your heart and live your best life, you inspire others to do the same.

-Taloa Walters

Summary & Testimony

My spiritual journey is unique, specific and miraculous for me, yet each and every person has their own spiritual journey to travel. My book Spirit Freedom is the path I've taken in my life. I believe with all my heart that in sharing my personal experiences and stories of my spiritual journey with you that the strategies I've used may also be applied on your spiritual journey. Although the strategies may be similar, the outcome will always be unique, personal and miraculous for you.

I've finally had the courage to write Spirit Freedom, and it is my witness to the world that our Heavenly Father lives. He is real and that He loves me and all His spirit children who have ever lived, presently live on the earth now and who are yet to be born in the future! In His unconditional love for us, He sent His Begotten Son, Jesus Christ who possessed power to sacrifice His life and atoned for our sins so that we could all return to our Heavenly Home through repentance and being baptised into His Church. I further witness that Jesus Christ's doctrine, priesthood authority and church once organised during His personal ministry approximately 30 AD is contained in the Restored Gospel, The Church of Jesus Christ of Latter Day Saints. I know that

Joseph Smith did see our Heavenly Father and Jesus Christ in the First Vision and was instrumental in restoring The Church of Jesus Christ of Latter Day Saints on the 6th of April 1830, allowing all of Heavenly Father's spirit children the opportunity to understand the Eternal Plan of Happiness, and receive all saving ordinances on the pathway back to our Heavenly Home. The Church of Jesus Christ of Latter Day Saints is led by Jesus Christ through revelation to a living prophet today, President Russell M. Nelson, authorised by Him to lead His church in preparation for His Second Coming More knowledge and information is found on the following link, https://www.churchofjesuschrist.org/?lang=eng and from studying the Book of Mormon, another testament of Jesus Christ along with the Holy Bible, the Doctrine and Covenants and the Pearl of Great Price. The most priceless promise and gift I could share with you is that when you pray sincerely to know that these things are true, through the power of the Holy Ghost, you will come to know, as I know, that these truths are true. It will change your life, your perspective on life and choices you make, empowering you to have Spirit Freedom and reach the potential our Heavenly Father has designed for you through His unconditional and eternal love for you. I share this personal witness and testimony because of my love for you all, in the name of our Saviour, and Redeemer, Jesus Christ, Amen.

Testimonials

It is refreshing to read a book that is filled with experiences of personal growth, faith in times of trial, love for Heavenly Father and commitment to the gospel of Jesus Christ all rolled into one. Taloa Walters understands what it means to endure, and each page testifies of that life lesson.

A remarkable testimony and very inspiring.

Valentina Croft

We have ALL been through trials. Tell me who hasn't. The purpose in life is to learn from our experiences and make the best of them. Taloa did an amazing job sharing her journey to find peace and happiness while growing closer to our Heavenly Father. The tools she teaches can help us find peace amidst trials.

Korban and Lani Blackburn

I'm extremely impressed with how Taloa captured my attention from the get-go. I really felt the spirit when reading and found that a lot of what was mentioned resonated with me on different levels. This book has inspired me to try the methods suggested to stay positive and endure to the end. I'm grateful that I was given the opportunity to read this beautiful piece of work. I'm truly touched by Taloa's life experience, and the example she sets is something I acquire to be like someday. I can see how this would benefit so many people; it is a book of strengthening both the spiritual and mental aspect of your existence. Thank you for this experience; I am blessed to call you my friend and my sister.

Priscilla Pupuke

It has been an honour to have grown up with this amazing, inspirational, spiritual, honest, hardworking, talented and patient woman, mother, entrepreneur, scholar, musician, baker and now author.

When Taloa told me that she was writing a book – I was extremely excited for her. I asked her to please, please, please make sure she saves a copy for me.

I am very proud of Taloa, and the great example she is to all who know her.

We are now blessed with the opportunity to read about this lovely lady's life journey and learn from the many life experiences and life lessons taught in her book. I agree with Taloa, that if we trust and centre our lives around our Heavenly Father and Jesus Christ, where all things are possible, our lives will be truly blessed.

Much alofas and congratulations Taloa on your wonderful book, "Spirit Freedom".

Si'i Warbin

Testimonials

This book starts with details that pull at the heartstrings of any family member and highlight the strength required by all in travelling their own journeys. I have always considered my eldest sister as a rock (solid and steadfast) and to now understand some of the struggles she has had to face in order to find spirit freedom. We have our own pitfalls and hardships to maneuver, our own trials and tribulations to overcome, our own dragons to slay and demons to vanquish but to find spirit freedom we must always fortify our spirits. I hope and pray that your read of this book opens doors and windows to your spirit freedom.

Petaia Solitua

Taloa is a special lady who has blessed not only my life but all those who have the privilege of coming into contact with her.

Having known Taloa for over 30 years, I have witnessed first-hand her love and dedication to our Saviour Jesus Christ. Taloa's shining example of Christ-like love to all those she meets, her dedication to living the gospel, her faithfulness, humility and unconditional love is a testimony to me.

Taloa is a true disciple of Jesus Christ, and I pray that you may feel of that love through reading this book.

Tia Corboba

References

Amerland, D. (2019). The Neuroscience of Self-Reflection - The Sniper Mind. Retrieved from https://thesnipermind.com/blog/the-neuroscience-of-self-reflection.html

Australian Institute of Health and Welfare (2019). The health of Australia's prisoners 2018. Cat. no. PHE 246. Canberra: AIHW Retrieved from https://www.aihw.gov.au/getmedia/2e92f007-453d-48a1-9c6b-4c9531cf0371/aihw-phe-246.pdf.aspx?inline=true

AZ quotes. (2020). A-Z quotes for all occasions. Retrieved from https://www.azquotes.com/

Child Family Community Australia (CFCA). (2020). Child abuse. Retrieved from https://aifs.gov.au/cfca/bibliography/child-sexual-abuse

The Church of Jesus Christ of Latter Day Saints (LDS). (2020). Worldwide Statistics. News. Retrieved from https://newsroom.churchofjesuschrist.org/facts-and-statistics/country/www.mormonnews.lv/#

The Church of Jesus Christ of Latter Day Saints (LDS). (2020). Newsroom. The Restoration of the Fullness of the Gospel of Jesus Christ. Retrieved from https://newsroom.churchofjesuschrist.org/multimedia/file/restoration-proclamation-2020-april.pdf

The Church of Jesus Christ of Latter Day Saints (LDS). (2000). The Relief Society Declaration. The Latter Day Saint Woman: The Woman's Manual, Part A. Retrieved from https://www.churchofjesuschrist.org/study/manual/the-latter-day-saint-woman-basic-manual-for-women-part-a/the-relief-society-declaration?lang=eng

Eyring, H. B. (2007). Coming unto Christ. General Conference. True to the Faith: From the Sermons and Discourses of David O. McKay, *comp. Llewelyn R. McKay [1966], 244).* Retrieved from https://www.churchofjesuschrist.org/study/new-era/2007/04/coming-unto-christ?lang=eng

Hinckley, G.B. (2016). Teachings of Presidents of the Church: Gordon B. Hinckley. Retrieved from https://www.churchofjesuschrist.org/study/manual/teachings-of-presidents-of-the-church-gordon-b-hinckley/chapter-1-the-restoration-of-the-gospel-the-dawning-of-a-brighter-day?lang=eng

Hinckley, G. B. (2017). Quotes by Gordon B. Hinckley. Goodreads. Retrieved from https://www.goodreads.com/quotes/147776-our-lives-are-the-only-meaningful-expression-of-what-we

Hinckley, G. B. (2020). Quotes by Gordon B. Hinckley. Goodreads. Retrieved from https://www.goodreads.com/quotes/65440-generally-speaking-the-most-miserable-people-i-know-are-those

Holland, P. T. (1987). One Needful Thing. Becoming Women of Faith in Christ. General Conference. Retrieved from https://www.churchofjesuschrist.org/study/ensign/1987/10/one-thing-needful-becoming-women-of-greater-faith-in-christ?lang=eng

Idlehearts (2020). Quotes by Ezra Taft Benson. Retrieved from https://www.idlehearts.com/quotes/author/ezra-taft-benson Kopischke, E. W. (2013). Being Accepted of the Lord. General Conference. Retrieved from https://www.churchofjesuschrist.org/study/general-conference/2013/04/being-accepted-of-the-lord?lang=eng

Luttrell, M. (2020). John Quincy Adams perfectly defined leadership. The North Bay Business Journal. Retrieved from https://legacy.

References

northbaybusinessjournal.com/industrynews/4180440-181/john-quincy-adams-perfectly-defined

Manes, E. (2013). The Power of Music: Pioneering Discoveries in the New Science of Song. Retrieved from https://www.bloomsbury.com/us/the-power-of-music-9780802778284/

McConkie, C. F. (2018). LDS apostle: Totally False that Suicide Leads to Permanent Hell. Deseret News. Retrieved from https://www.deseret.com/2018/7/2/20648210/lds-apostle-totally-false-that-suicide-leads-to-permanent-hell

Mendes, Anthony (1996). *Inspiring Commitment : How to Win Employee Loyalty in Chaotic Times.* Irwin Professional Pub, Chicago

Miles, M. Lifeology. (2020). EQ. Emotional Intelligence. Retrieved from https://wearelifeology.com/services/eq/

Millet, R.L. (2001) What Mormons believe about Jesus Christ. Harvard Divinity School. March, 2001. Retrieved from https://newsroom.churchofjesuschrist.org/article/what-mormons-believe-about-jesus-christ

Mission Australia. (2019). Mission Australia Youth Infographic 2019. Retrieved from https://www.missionaustralia.com.au/publications/youth-survey

Morin, A. (2014). 7 Scientifically Proven Benefits of Gratitude That Will Motivate you to Give Thanks Year – Round. Psychology Today. Retrieved from https://www.psychologytoday.com/au/blog/what-mentally-strong-people-dont-do/201504/7-scientifically-proven-benefits-gratitude

National Public Radio (NPR). (2011). 'The Power Of Music' To Affect The Brain: NPR. Author interviews. Retrieved from https://www.npr.org/2011/06/01/136859090/the-power-of-music-to-affect-the-brain#:~:text='The%20Power%20Of%20Music'%20To%20Affect%20The%20Brain%20%3A%20NPR&text='The%20Power%20Of%20Music'%20To%20Affect%20The%20Brain%20Science%20all,Parkinson's%20disease%20or%20a%20stroke.

Nelson, R.M. (2008). The Power and Protection of Worthy Music. Church Education System Address at Brigham Young University. Retrieved from https://www.churchofjesuschrist.org/study/ensign/2009/12/the-power-and-protection-of-worthy-music?lang=eng

Nelson, R.M. (2014). Will you choose to increase in learning? Church Education system address on September 8, 2013. Retrieved from https://www.churchofjesuschrist.org/study/new-era/2014/09/will-you-choose-to-increase-in-learning?lang=eng

Oxford Learner's Dictionaries. (2020). EQ- Emotional Intelligence. Retrieved from https://www.oxfordlearnersdictionaries.com/definition/english/emotional-intelligence

Packer, B. K. (2009) Prayers and Promptings. General Conference, October 2009, Retrieved from https://www.thechurchnews.com/archives/2009-10-03/president-boyd-k-packer-prayer-and-promptings-69375

Parkin, B. D. (2007). Gratitude: A Path to Happiness. General Conference speech. https://www.churchofjesuschrist.org/study/general-conference/2007/04/gratitude-a-path-to-happiness?lang=eng

Rosenberg, Matt. (2019). A List of Current Communist Countries in the World Post-Soviet Communism Is on the Wane. Thoughtco. Retrieved from: https://www.thoughtco.com/communist-countries-overview-1435178

Scott, Richard G. (1992). Healing the Tragic Scars of Abuse. April General Conference. Retrieved from https://www.churchofjesuschrist.org/study/general-conference/1992/04/healing-the-tragic-scars-of-abuse?lang=eng

Smith, T. (2010). Commitment: Its Purpose and Power. Retrieved from http://www.littlethingsmatter.com/blog/2010/07/15/commitment-its-purpose-and-power/

Smith, J (2011) Teachings of the prophets: Joseph Smith. Chapter 17: The Great Plan of Salvation. Retrieved from https://www.churchofjesuschrist.org/study/manual/teachings-joseph-smith/chapter-17?lang=eng

References

Snow, S. (2001). Gratitude. Joseph F. Smith. Gospel Principles, 5th Edition. [1939]262. Retrieved from https://www.churchofjesuschrist.org/study/general-conference/2001/10/gratitude?lang=eng

Wirthlin, J. B. (2000). Finding a Safe Harbor. General Conference April 2000. Retrieved from https://www.churchofjesuschrist.org/study/general-conference/2000/04/finding-a-safe-harbor?lang=eng

Wirthlin, J. B. (2006). The Abundant Life. General Conference April 2006. Retrieved from https://www.churchofjesuschrist.org/study/general-conference/2006/04/the-abundant-life?lang=eng

World Health Organization. (2020). Child Maltreatment. Newsroom. Fact Sheet. Retrieved from https://www.who.int/news-room/fact-sheets/detail/child-maltreatment

World Health Organization. (2020). Suicide. Newsroom. Fact sheet. Retrieved from https://www.who.int/news-room/fact-sheets/detail/suicide Young, B. (2012). Reaching Out: A View on Interfaith Respect. Retrieved from https://newsroom.churchofjesuschrist.org/article/reaching-out-expansive-view-interfaith-respect#_ftn5

Wixon, R. M. (2013) The Influence of Music. For the strength of youth address. Retrieved from https://www.churchofjesuschrist.org/study/new-era/2013/09/the-influence-of-music?lang=eng

World population Review. (2020). Communist Countries Population. Retrieved from http://worldpopulationreview.com/countries/communist-countries/

APPENDICES

Affirmations and Essential Oils (Self Help And Healing)

Chapters

1. Awaken

   Suggested Affirmation/Essential Oils
   - My Heavenly Father loves me, I am His Spirit (son/daughter) - Arborvitae oil for Divine Grace/Rose oil of Divine Love
   - My Heavenly Father answers my prayers and helps me succeed in life – Lavender oil of Communication

2. Potential

   Suggested Affirmation/Essential Oils
   - I know my purpose here on earth and embrace it with all my heart – Roman Chamomile oil of

spiritual purpose/Rosemary oil of Knowledge and Transition
- I live the Plan of Happiness and experience Joy each day – Frankincense oil of Truth

3. Choice

Suggested Affirmation/Essential Oils
- I choose eternal happiness and joy each day – Lemon oil of Focus
- I choose Heavenly Father's plan for me because He knows what's best for me – Oregano oil of Humility

4. Power

Suggested Affirmation/Essential Oils
- I embrace worthy music to express divine devotion – Marjoram oil of Connection
- Worthy music empowers and protects me – Geranium oil of Love and Trust/Ginger oil of Empowerment

5. Connect

Suggested Affirmation/Essential Oils
- I am connected to my spirit and also to the Holy Ghost for guidance and direction – Sandalwood oil of Sacred Devotion
- I am open to Heavenly guidance to understand my spirit – Cilantro oil of Releasing Control

6. Grateful

Suggested Affirmation/Essential Oils
- I am grateful for all that I have experienced and everything I will experience today and in the future – Thyme oil of Releasing and Forgiving
- I am abundant in love, light, hope and happiness – Eucalyptus oil of Wellbeing/Melissa oil of Light

Affirmations and Essential Oils (Self Help And Healing)

7. Vision
Suggested Affirmation/Essential Oils
- I have vision of abundance, prosperity and freedom in every aspect of my life – Peppermint oil of a Buoyant Heart/ Wild Orange oil of Abundance
- I embrace love, knowledge and beauty all around me to lift and attract more abundance – Lime oil of Zest for Life/Clary Sage oil of Clarity and Vision

8. Discover
Suggested Affirmation/Essential Oils
- I thrive on personal development and re-discovering myself daily to excel in every aspect of life and have inner peace and joy – Cassia oil of Self-assurance
- I am enough and loved for who I am each day – Bergamot oil of Self-acceptance

9. Reflect
Suggested Affirmation/Essential Oils
- I feel exhilarated when I reflect on positive experiences to have spiritual strength and agility – Spearmint oil of Refreshment
- I feel energy and creativity flow through me to achieve goals and dreams – Tangerine oil of Cheer and Creativity

10. Endure
Suggested Affirmation/Essential Oils
- I have endurance and vitality to conquer all things with my Heavenly Father's love and protection – Basil oil of Renewal
- I am empowered by divine intervention of love, hope and peace each day – Birch oil of Support

11. Voice

    Suggested Affirmation/Essential Oils
- I have confidence in expressing my voice on matters that are of great value to me in a positive and uplifting way! – Lavender oil of Communication.
- I voice and express spiritual knowledge to create transition and elevation to higher levels of tranquillity, vibration, attraction and brilliance! – Rosemary oil of Knowledge and Transition

12. Inspire

    Suggested Affirmation/Essential Oils
- I inspire others to live their best life, growing and developing in my own life at the same time! – Cedar oil of Community/ Birch oil of Support
- I am a vessel in our Heavenly Father's hands to radiate his love, hope and peace to everyone I come in contact with! – Wintergreen oil of Surrender/ Bergamot oil of Self-acceptance/Wild orange oil of Abundance

Affirmations and Essential Oils (Self Help And Healing)

VISION BOARD

Church Service

Health & Wellness

Business Leader

Music Studio for creative expression

Writer

Open Global school for Financial and Investment Education

Dream Car

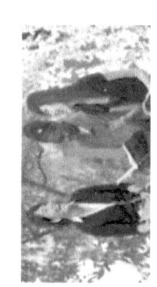
PHD Philosophy

Bakery

Financial Freedom/ Trillion Dollars

Dream House

Taloa Walters

For Massage

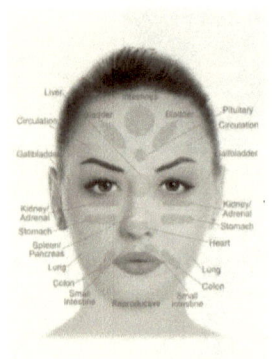

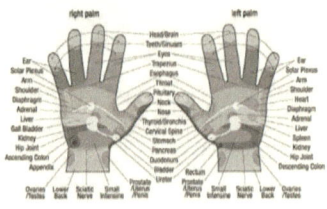

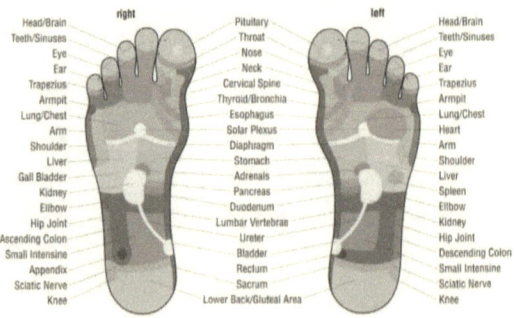

Affirmations and Essential Oils (Self Help And Healing)

Worthy Music

Hymns https://www.churchofjesuschrist.org/music/library/hymns?lang=eng

Children's Song Book https://www.churchofjesuschrist.org/music/library/childrens-songbook?lang=eng

Classical Music Selection https://www.youtube.com/watch?v=GgYm2uHvQbU
https://www.youtube.com/watch?v=mB-QXgtoItA

Handel's Messiah https://www.youtube.com/watch?v=7hhcURZVx5k

Relaxation music https://www.youtube.com/watch?v=1zUAth9I184

Come unto Christ https://www.youtube.com/watch?v=uUAsy5ReP8Y&list=RDuUAsy5ReP8Y&start_radio=1

Glorious https://www.youtube.com/watch?v=nomxXk6Q1rk&list=RDuUAsy5ReP8Y&index=4

Peace in Christ https://www.youtube.com/watch?v=R46J-GjbRWA

When someone cares https://www.youtube.com/watch?v=libPgjKWvOk

I will be what I believe https://www.youtube.com/watch?v=3PIyzaKkzTQ

A Child's Prayer https://www.youtube.com/watch?v=RboDtFCtknM

I'm still here https://www.youtube.com/watch?v=RboDtFCtknM

Latter Day Saints arrangements of uplifting songs https://www.youtube.com/watch?v=X6Mtpk4jeVA&list=PL49dKqcX401FD1qEaLKa8z1G4hiUAaJ3B

Instrumental music https://www.youtube.com/watch?v=CHV6BjuQOZQ&list=PL49dKqcX401FD1qEaLKa8z1G4hiUAaJ3B&index=2
https://www.youtube.com/watch?v=UVUwgxuDb9A&list=PL49dKqcX401FD1qEaLKa8z1G4hiUAaJ3B&index=4

Orchestral music https://www.youtube.com/watch?v=S7VxHhZbW50

Relaxation, meditation and massage music https://www.youtube.com/watch?v=2OEL4P1Rz04
https://www.youtube.com/watch?v=9uIk_91GQYI

Afterword

Thank you for sharing in my spiritual journey by reading Spirit Freedom. I hope that through my personal experiences, you may come to relate, understand and be guided on your own journey. As I shared throughout my book, I hope you will sincerely pray to know Heavenly Father's love for you, apply that love as your guide, study scriptures for divine knowledge, insights and treasures, and trust Him to help you live the life you are meant to live. Trust that as you do this, your life will be filled with miracles, rich experiences and a resolve that as you continue following your Saviour and older brother, Jesus Christ's example, doing all you can, assurance of an eternal life of ultimate happiness, joy, love and peace beyond this mortal life will be yours.

Acknowledgements

I'm eternally grateful to our Heavenly Father, Jesus Christ and the Holy Ghost for their love, inspiration and guidance throughout my life, particularly in writing, Spirit Freedom. I am also grateful to my parents, grandparents, siblings, eternal companion and my daughters for their constant love, patience and support. I'm thankful to all my friends for their friendship and insights. I am truly grateful to all my spiritual mentors, including President Russell M Nelson and The Church of Jesus Christ of Latter Day Saints, who have been my spiritual global international family. I'm thankful to all my professional connections for sharing knowledge, life experiences and expertise that have contributed to inspiring me to write Spirit Freedom! This also includes Tanya and Cassile at A1 Health Energy Workz and their wonderful community, Doterra Essential Oils, Early Childhood Education and Care community, and Andrey Khovratov and the New Economic Evolution of the World community. I particularly would like to thank Natasa Denman and the Ultimate 48 Hour Author team for helping me achieve my dream to become a published author sharing my story in Spirit Freedom. Love and gratitude to you all in sharing this spiritual journey with me!

About the Author

Taloa Walters was born in Auckland, New Zealand to faithful Latter Day Saint parents, Tuputala and Siaunofo Solitua. She is of Samoan, German and Chinese cultural background. After her spiritual and life-changing experience at the age of seven, a few years later, on December 23, 1982, after her eleventh birthday, she moved with her family to Australia. With a fresh new start, family life in Sydney was life-saving and filled with abundance. Taloa trusted in her Heavenly Father, guided by His love throughout her childhood and teenage experiences utilising the power of worthy music. Her faith and love of our Heavenly Father and Jesus Christ increased through her personal study of his doctrines in the scriptures, being mentored and influenced by the faith and example of others, raising her four daughters, Siona, Tiara, Kirra and Elena, caring for her mother, Siaunofo and spiritually supporting her eleven siblings and their extended families. Taloa currently lives in Sydney and continues to live her life's purpose, sharing her faith and serving within her family, her church community as a member of The Church of Jesus Christ of Latter Day Saints and sharing knowledge in other fields of health and wellness, early childhood education and care, life coaching and finance, business and investing literacy.

Taloa Walters studied at Brigham Young University Hawaii, graduating with an Associate Degree in Music Instrumental and

Taloa Walters

Bachelor Degree in Science, Special Education in 2000. Later in 2019, Taloa received her Master in Education degree in Early Childhood Education and Care for research from Torrens University, Australia. Taloa also has certifications in Relaxation Massage, Grandmaster Reiki, Neurological Linguistic Programming, Applied Kinesiology, Professional Life Coaching and Business Management. She is currently working on her proposal for a Doctorate Degree in Philosophy, emphasising the importance of spiritual development, ultimately motivating all other areas of development in our lives. She is also sharing an opportunity within the fields of financial and investment knowledge using Spirit Freedom as the foundation for accessing financial freedom!

Taloa Walters may be contacted at taloaw@gmail.com for any questions. You may also reach her in Sydney, Australia on mobile, +61 403115756 or on her website at www.taloawalters.com

Taloa Walters

is enthusiastic, fun, passionate and excited about connecting and networking with people! As a mother to 4 beautiful daughters and an aunty to over 40 amazing nieces and nephews, Taloa is passionate about helping children connect with their true identity and divine potential! Grateful for Spirit Freedom and believes in making the most of everyday we live on this earth! A trusted expert on holistic, positive, natural, health and wellness approaches to enrich and empower people to embrace a growth mindset, reach their ultimate potential, excel in their talents and live their dreams! She is an entrepreneur with several years of experience within various home businesses in food, family daycare, promoting health products, music, energy healing, massage relaxation, as well as financial and investment education.

The Author of Spirit Freedom, Taloa speaks on the following topics:

- Shares knowledge and concepts of how to develop spirituality as a solid foundation for success in all areas of life!

- Shares step by step strategies on how to unlock unlimited spiritual potential to live a life of intention!

- Shares daily practices on how to draw on divine heavenly powers and connect with inner powers to attract love, hope, peace and happiness in life and to sustain that forever!

✉ taloaw@gmail.com or
📞 0403115756

to enquire about engaging **Taloa** as a speaker at your next event.

www.ingramcontent.com/pod-product-compliance
Lightning Source LLC
Chambersburg PA
CBHW021151080526
44588CB00008B/299